THIS BOOK IS DEDICATED TO
GAITRI M.M. SINGH
AND
MANMEET WIRK

THE LUNAR NODES

CRISIS
AND
REDEMPTION

KOMILLA SUTTON

The Wessex Astrologer Ltd

Published in England in 2001 by
The Wessex Astrologer Ltd
PO Box 9307
Swanage
BH19 9BF
England
for a full list of our titles please go to www.wessexastrologer.com

ISBN 1902405099

Cover art © Paul F. Newman 2001

A catalogue record for this book is available at the British Library

Acknowledgements

I'd like to thank the following people for their help and support:

Paul F. Newman for his artistic sketches and the excellent editing

Margaret Cahill for being the best publisher

Jim Cahill for being a technical Guru

Liz Grantham-Hill for her practical support

Viv Lelyweld for her love and guidance

Andrew Foss for being my karmic friend

Emily and Bernard Renaud for lending me their lakeside villa for writing this book

Diana Perez for her friendship

My brother Kuldip Wirk without whose help and support I would not have been where I am today

Dr. Ajit Sinha for introducing me to the wonderful world of astrology

And finally, to the embodiment of my positive karma of past lives, Naniji, my uncle M.M Singh and my mom

Also by Komilla Sutton

The Nakshatras - The Stars Beyond the Zodiac
The Essentials of Vedic Astrology
Lunar Nodes - Crisis and Redemption
Personal Panchanga and the Five Sources of Light
Vedic Love Signs
Indian Astrology

Komilla Sutton teaches all over the world and you can check her itinerary through her website at
www.komilla.com

CONTENTS

1

Introducing Rahu Ketu

This book is devoted to bringing forth new material to help you understand Rahu and Ketu, the Lunar Nodes, in the birth chart. They are the karmic axis of our lives: the invisible link between past lives and the psychological dilemmas of the present. They represent the hidden side of human nature, our psychological characters, the interplay of the shadows within us - both good and bad - our fears, sorrows, unfulfilled desires, doubts, unhappiness, strengths and weaknesses. A connection has to be established between the practicalities of life and the deep mysteries of our past. Through this journey, you will not only discover yourself but will be able to lead life with strength rather than weakness.

What are Rahu and Ketu?

Rahu Ketu is the Sanskrit name given collectively to the Nodes of the Moon: Rahu is the North Node and Ketu is the South Node, but they are often referred to jointly as Rahu Ketu. They are not physical bodies, but the two points at which the orbit of the Moon intersects the ecliptic or the apparent path of the Sun around the Earth. When the Moon is moving from south to north and intersects the ecliptic, that point is called Rahu or the North Node. When the Moon passes from north to south, the intersection is called Ketu or the South Node. When the Moon intersects the apparent path of the Sun, it disturbs the electromagnetic field and this can create eclipses, which are considered full of occult significance. The Moon crosses this intersection every thirteen days, but eclipses only occur when the Sun, Earth and Moon are in particular alignment. A solar eclipse occurs during the New Moon when the Sun is in exact alignment with the Earth and Moon, and the Moon is +/- 18 degrees from the nodes. From the Earth's point of view, the Moon's shadow falls on the Sun and we are momentarily in darkness. A lunar eclipse happens when the Earth is exactly

Solar Eclipse

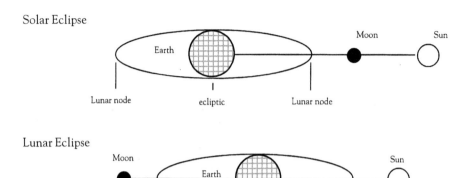

Lunar Eclipse

aligned between a Full Moon and the Sun, and the Moon is +/- 11 degrees from the nodal position. The light to the Moon is then blocked and we see just its ghostly shadow. The eclipses follow the axis of the transiting lunar nodes, so if for example they are transiting the Taurus/Scorpio axis, that is where the eclipses will occur. You can find out where the eclipses were happening around the time of your birth by studying the positions of Rahu and Ketu on your natal chart. Rahu and Ketu move in a retrograde motion, taking 18 years to complete one cycle of the zodiac and staying in one sign for approximately 18 months. The nodes indicate the precise point of harmony with the three most important influences in our life- the Sun, the Earth and the Moon. This relationship plays an important part in the unfolding of individual consciousness. The symbol of Rahu and Ketu is the serpent and they represent the Kundalini Shakti (power).

The Importance of the Nodes in Vedic Astrology

Rahu and Ketu are the key to unlocking the relationship of the soul with its past life. They have been given the status of planets to emphasise their significance and are known as *chayya grahas* (shadow planets). They have no substance and are physically non-existent as they are points in the ecliptic, yet their influence is full of potency and spiritual significance. The nodes represent polarities with a mission to churn up our lives in order to bring out the hidden potential and wisdom that has been gathered from the karma of previous lives. In keeping with their shadowy nature they work on a psychological level, but in both the mundane world and in spiritual life. Their function in the material realm urges us to redirect our desires: what is darkness to a person enmeshed in materialistic ambitions can be powerful spiritual energy for those on the path of moksha and spiritual enlightenment.

Rahu and Ketu represent our inner struggles. In the physical world we are accustomed to fighting external aggressors, but the nodes represent the internal battle between our own positive and negative forces. Exactly where this battle will manifest is indicated by the nodal axis. Taken together Rahu and Ketu represent both the best and worst aspects of our personality and they are in a continual struggle for supremacy. All of us have a darker side to our nature, which if left unchecked would create havoc within our lives. By trying to control it, we learn the true lesson of Rahu and Ketu and can express the illuminating side of both their natures.

Rahu, Ketu and the Eclipses

As Rahu and Ketu symbolically eclipse the Sun (consciousness) and the Moon (the mind), they have a great part to play in darkening our perspective in readiness for the bringing in of new light. They deal with the concept of death and re-birth, transformation and regeneration. During eclipses the light from the Luminaries is darkened creating powerfully psychic energies, pregnant with new information and occult power, which in turn leads to a rebirth of the Sun and the Moon after the eclipse has passed. The role of the nodes in this powerful alignment of Sun, Moon and Earth is to act as ultimate controllers of destiny. The Rahu Ketu axis in the birth chart represents your own personal eclipse point; how you struggle with the destiny imposed on you from your past life karma. These struggles bring about the flowering of your personality and enable you to overcome issues of the past. In a sense Rahu and Ketu can represent both restrictions and liberation.

The Sun represents the soul and the Moon its reflection - a reflection that is present in the mind of every individual. In a perfect state, both planets are timeless and unfettered by any physical restrictions, but Rahu and Ketu can cast a shadow over them. Just as the eclipse causes the light from the Sun or Moon to be blocked from us on Earth, so can the nodes create problems that make us feel we were born into a spiritual darkness. In the birth chart, the nodes control karma, giving us the impression that our lives/souls are no longer eternal but subject to the laws of the world. Thankfully this feeling is only temporary - in the same way that an eclipse is soon over, we are also sure to find our own light. We begin the search, cut through the shadows of the mind and start to embrace that light.

Karma and Rahu Ketu

The word karma literally means 'action'. Every action taken in our current, past and future lives is our karma. We choose from our previous karma the issues we wish to face in this life, both negative and positive: by addressing them now we give our souls the chance to mature and move towards their ultimate goal of enlightenment. Like beads on a necklace, previous lifetimes are interconnected by an invisible thread - which is Rahu Ketu. As the indicators and the Lords of Karma in the birth chart they represent the stumbling blocks which when overcome, eventually lead to liberation and maturity of the soul. Ketu deals with past Karma and Rahu with the need to create new karma.

The Myth of Naga Vasuki

There is a wonderful myth concerning Rahu Ketu, which illustrates beautifully how (and why) we are constantly pulled in two directions at once:

There was once a Great War between the gods and the demons for the control of the universe. Naga Vasuki was a demon serpent who ruled the Patala Loka, the underworld. At some point (and no doubt for his own motives) he decided he would help the gods in their search for Amrita, the nectar of immortality. He allowed the gods to tie his snake-like body around the spiritual mountain, Mandara, so it could be used as a rod to churn up the ocean during the course of the search. When they found the nectar the gods wanted to keep this great prize for themselves for they rightly felt the demons would only use it for personal and materialistic gratification. They plied the demons with wine, women and song to distract their attention, but they hadn't reckoned with wise Vasuki. He wasn't fooled by the gods' ploy and he slunk away to drink the nectar in secret. The Sun and the Moon discovered what he had done and complained to Lord Vishnu, creator of the Universe, who grew very angry at this deception. He threw a wheel called the Sudharshan Chakra at Vasuki and cut him in two, but of course Vasuki was now immortal as a result of drinking the Amrita and could not be killed. He remains in the skies as Rahu (the head) and Ketu (the body), a permanent reminder to the other planets (gods) that the darker side of life has to be defeated in the pursuit of immortality.

Lessons from the Mythology of Rahu Ketu

In ancient literature, important lessons were given in story form so that people could relate them to their own lives. We can see from this myth that the Sun and Moon became enemies of Rahu Ketu because they complained to Lord Vishnu about Vasuki; thus any conjunctions of Rahu Ketu with the Sun and Moon are full of esoteric and karmic significance. The myth of Naga Vasuki is very much an allegory of life. Without the help of Vasuki, the gods could not have found the secret of immortality and, in the same way, without understanding the lessons of Rahu and Ketu we humans cannot find our higher selves. Our inner emotions are like the ocean being churned, within which are treasures but also poisons and dangers. We have to learn to distinguish the precious from the dross to finally find Amrita - the secret of immortality or true happiness. The conflict is between our attachment to materialistic achievements (the domain of Rahu) and the liberation of the soul through eternal bliss and tranquillity (Ketu). Ketu is the significator in the chart for spiritual realisation. Vasuki wasn't taken in by the illusion that deceived the other demons - he wanted to achieve far more than they did, so he didn't do what was expected of him. Rahu is very ambitious with the necessary drive to achieve whatever it desires, but it is never satisfied. Ketu however is always there, reminding us that we have past life issues that have to be addressed, and that to ignore them means foregoing any real, spiritual progress. Ketu also represents the cycles of change in life - we can't always demand that life goes according to our own plans.

The story of Vasuki is also that of the serpent cut in half, which is an allegory of the way we are separated from our previous lives when we are born. As the umbilical cord is cut and we are separated from our mother, the soul also cuts away from the essential part of us, which is the source, our infinite connection to the past and our identification with eternity. In the same way as we keep an emotional connection with our mother, there remains an invisible link of the present to our past. Rahu (the present) is forever searching for its lost half, Ketu (the past) - we need to understand our past connections to become whole again. The story of Rahu Ketu is the severing of our body and soul, and once they reconnect, we become complete.

Kundalini

Rahu and Ketu indicate the kundalini, which is derived from the Sanskrit word *kundal* meaning a coil of rope similar to a snake lying coiled while resting. Kundalini also means coiling, spiralling and winding. It is a form of Durga or Shakti - the female power - and is the hidden power that lies dormant within us. As the kundalini awakens it starts to rise upwards against the gravitational pull in the same way that a snake spirals out of its coil. While the kundalini is dormant we remain unaware of our extra potential, the sleeping fire we are harbouring. The search for self-knowledge eventually brings us to a higher level of awareness, beyond the normal state of human consciousness, and the kundalini provides the link. As its energy changes from static to dynamic, a whole new inner world is opened to us. It one of hidden power, individual consciousness and links to past, present and future lives. The force of the dynamic kundalini rises through the psychic centers or the chakras of the body towards the sahasara or crown chakra. Here it is surrounded by a great light of consciousness that ends the separation of human from spiritual. When the kundalini is fully awakened, the soul becomes one with eternal consciousness.

The image of the kundalini rising against gravity is shown by the retrograde motion of Rahu Ketu. The other planets mostly travel forwards but Rahu Ketu always move backward against the trends and the forces of life. Rahu Ketu, when representing the static kundalini, indicate the power within us that can change the course of our destiny, but this power is untapped and static until awakened. The serpent in the coil sleeps with his head downwards. It is when the kundalini rises from a dormant to a dynamic state that most problems are created. As the head of the snake faces downwards the first experiences are of a more worldly nature. While the kundalini is awaking it is as yet unregulated and undirected to its true path. The lower kundalini can be destructive, and turning it from a downward to an upward flowing energy requires great care. Many Yogic practitioners try to waken the sleeping kundalini voluntarily, but one has to be careful in waking the sleeping serpent. It can bite us if we are unprepared and its venom can create psychological problems. Just as the snake charmer learns to play the right music for the snake to dance to his tune, we need knowledge and preparation to learn the control of this potent force within us. Interpreters have only tended to perceive Rahu Ketu as the destructive side of the kundalini, forgetting that its highly beneficial and positive side takes us to the highest level of perception. When we become masters of our Rahu Ketu energy, we are able to change the course of our life.

The Kundalini

In its static state the kundalini rests at the base of the spine (Muladhara chakra); it is represented by a sleeping snake coiled 3 ½ times around the Shiva Lingham (see picture). As it awakens, the kundalini rises in a ferocious fiery form through the chakras to meet its positive force that rests in the Sahasara or the crown chakra. Here it reaches its destination and brings about enlightenment.

2

The Rahu Personality -
The Compulsion to Experience Life

Rahu and Ketu together form the karmic axis but they have distinct individual features. When studying your chart, you need to study Rahu and Ketu separately and then the axis.

Rahu is the projection of past life issues onto today's landscape. Rahu becomes obsessed with externalising past life wishes through present experiences, and in keeping with its shadowy nature this projection is in the mind. Many interpretations show only the negative side of Rahu - like the fiery and destructive force of the arising kundalini, Rahu on its own, without due knowledge of its power, is usually perceived as similarly dangerous, but this is seeing just half the picture. Rahu energy, like the kundalini, needs to be trained and disciplined. Once this is achieved it has the capacity to defy both gravity and convention, and make immense changes to the individual psyche. While you are studying Rahu, always remember its negativity as well as its great occult power and its supreme ability to give you real results in life both materially and spiritually.

In the horoscope, Rahu is at its best when alone in the house it is occupying as conjunctions with other planets will affect their qualities. Rahu with malefics like Saturn, Mars and the Sun will become even more malefic, and with benefics it can trade their good points for its own negative ones.

Identifying with the Subconscious
Rahu forms the head part of the celestial snake and therefore it has no body. In one sense this identifies it as the heartless intellectual, the thinker who forgets to feel and be in touch with his emotional nature. But in occult terminology, the lower brain - which is the organ of the subconscious mind - is also known as the serpent brain and it is here that the ego resides. If the ego gets out of control

the mind can develop negative thoughts, leading to fear or phobias; a positive understanding of the subconscious allows one to overcome that fear and to reach spiritual realisation by connecting to the soul's ultimate mission.

Meet Mr. Ambition

Rahu and ambition go hand in hand. As Vasuki, Rahu managed to take the nectar from the gods against all the odds, and he recognises no obstacles in his way. The position of Rahu on your birth chart indicates where you will strive hardest to achieve perfection. While lack of achievement can create immense dissatisfactions, an important fact to remember is that you must try to limit your ambitions. Always look back to see what you have achieved and take satisfaction in those accomplishments. Rahu's attitude after climbing Mount Everest would be to plan to fly to Mars, so if one climbed the highest peak in the world Rahu would still bring a feeling of failure because of the inability to have also reached Mars. This sense of dissatisfaction can become a problem if you do not address it immediately.

The Great Politician

Rahu's influence is that of a planner, manipulator and strategist. To be a good politician, you need to have a strong Rahu. It gives the ability to work in the shadows, make plans and create strategies that others find difficult to deal with. On the negative side Rahu can be a great manipulator.

Experiencing Life at Super Intensity

Rahu experiences life to the full. It is intense, driven and compulsive and when in full flow there is absolutely nothing that can come in its way. Whether its aim is spiritual or material Rahu will show the same intensity in every pursuit.

Heaven and Earth

The sleeping kundalini faces downwards, so the first experiences of Rahu will be with the world below your own. It can take you on a journey through the darker realms of existence, from drug addiction, crime and negativity, then upwards towards the highest spiritual teachings. Valmiki, who wrote the great Indian Epic *Ramayana*, was a robber and a bandit and his transformation into the saint who wrote such deep philosophies shows the magic of Rahu. There can be a deeply negative side as long as an individual looks downward, but once they begin to look towards heaven, they have the ability to turn their life around and achieve the impossible.

Life in the Shadows
Because it is shadowy in nature, with no substance or grounding, Rahu is only aware of its connection to Ketu on a subconscious level. In reality it acts alone searching for its hidden mate.

Swimming Against the Tide
The Rahu energy is like a salmon - always running against the flow. Rahu's retrograde motion suggests that it does not follow the movement the other planets take, and it likes to shock. If Rahu is placed in the 7th house, you may be happy to marry someone your parents do not approve of. Similarly if it is placed in the 9th, you may be attracted to ideas and philosophies that shock the traditionalist.

The Outsider
Rahu is an outsider. He is the only demon among the gods, so his role in your life will be to look at things from an outsider's perspective. If you are strongly ruled by Rahu, you may feel like an outsider yourself. This can sometimes produce the urge to annoy those who do not accept you, or even to be vengeful in order to show your power. This is something you must learn to overcome.

Patterns of Dissatisfaction and Disappointment
Rahu projects past life needs into this life. It wishes to satisfy all the unfulfilled desires of a previous life and so its action is of a relentless search that has no beginning or end. Rahu's position in your chart will highlight this area of dissatisfaction. As long as Rahu continues making this search in the purely material realm, the result is likely to end in disappointment and dissatisfaction. To change this trend you have to realise the patterns you are creating in the subconscious, then slowly try to break with them.

The Fears Created by Rahu
The fears created by Rahu are behaviour patterns that have to be broken as you learn to tame the serpent. To avoid a life driven by fear and dissatisfaction, they need to be dealt with as they come up, or they may turn into deep-rooted phobias. They are irrational and come from nowhere, so the more you try to rationalize their impact, the worse they become. When you finally surrender to this apparent force of darkness, you will find that the fear will disappear, but it needs the spiritual practice of control over the mind and a sense of detachment from the world. This is why Rahu's impact is so great; the fears it creates are greatly magnified if it is placed with either Moon or Mercury - the planets of the mind.

Death, Transformation and Rebirth

There is a hymn that refers to Rahu being shaped like a snake. Snakes are given great importance in vedic mythology as Lord Shiva has a snake around his neck and Lord Vishnu's throne was Shesh Naga - the Eternal Serpent. Shesh Naga represents the cycles of time and space which are the seeds of cosmic creation. The Nagas are shaped like snakes but stand upright. They are wise, highly evolved beings, whose wisdom can be used for both good and bad. The Naga shedding his skin symbolises transformation, death and re-birth, so the snakes in vedic literature remind people of their mortality.

The 'devouring of the Sun and Moon' occurs when Rahu eclipses the luminaries. This shows the important part Rahu has to play in changing the course of our life. The Sun and Moon are Royal planets under whose dictates the universe and life on earth revolves, but Rahu can darken this light and therefore control the processes of life. The Sun is the Soul and the Moon is the Mind, and when eclipsed they go through transformation, death and regeneration.

Shakti or the Untapped Power Within

Rahu's function is to connect to the shakti, the feminine, passive power within us which needs masculine power to become active. Once that connection is made a person is said to be siddha or powerful; he has control over his senses and this makes him immensely powerful spiritually. The diligence and work involved in gaining control is associated with the 6th house, so to become siddha we have to overcome the obstacles presented in daily life. There are 6 shaktis that help in the process of evolution:

- Parashakti - power represented by heat and light (Sun)
- Gyana Shakti - power though knowledge and wisdom
- Icchashakti - will power
- Kriya Shakti - power of creative action
- Kundalini Shakti - the latent power within us
- Matrakashati - power of speech, letters and music

Positive Force

Rahu is the colour of Aakash, which means sky or that which pervades all space, and is usually called the colour of the gods. This godly connection indicates that while Rahu is essentially malefic, it is in the end very good for us. It creates situations through which we grow, understand and accept our personalities. Rahu in the birth chart creates disturbances only so that we may come into contact with our essential mysterious quality. While the other gods of Hindu mythology have different antagonists to fight, our main antagonist is Rahu, the hidden urges that restrict our growth. By conquering and overpowering these negative forces we are able to be at one with Aakash, the celestial electricity that connects us to the source.

The Temptations of Rahu

Rahu tempts us from the path of our dharmic past onto the road of self-destruction, but it has a very definite purpose for doing so. It wants us to taste and feel everything so that when the senses have been fully satiated we turn again on the path of self-realisation and find true enlightenment. On the physical plane Rahu gives an insatiable desire to achieve and conquer, but once a pinnacle of achievement has been reached we realise that success does not bring happiness and that we were in fact chasing an illusion. There are many cults in India which preach satiation of all mundane and carnal desires in order to learn the fundamental lesson that fulfilment of desires does not bring true happiness.

Saturn as the Alter-Ego

Rahu behaves like Saturn, whose restrictions direct the soul back to its true purpose in life. It works on the material level causing immense pain as illusions are shattered. It forces us to come face to face with our negative karma creating struggles between us and our desires and passions so that we can be released from them. Rahu gives us material fulfilment allowing us to achieve our ambitions, but it causes psychological dissatisfaction because it highlights the emptiness within. Both Rahu and Saturn shape and change our destiny - one on the material level and the other on the psychological.

Disciplining the Powers during the Dashas

Rahu has an 18-year life cycle in the Vimshottari Dasha system and its strong personality dominates during this dasha. The Rahu Dasha can be like a roller coaster; you experience both the highs and lows of life. One thing is certain; it will never be a boring experience! The strong Rahu can make this a time of high achievement but one needs to learn how pacify its fiery nature to make it more benefic. The key to enjoying a Rahu dasha is to keep its desires and expressions in control - try to stay grounded and control the urge to go that extra step. When Rahu is conjunct malefic planets (Saturn, Sun, Mars), it can become very fierce and intense, for the malefic planets increase this effect and are the ones determined to succeed regardless of any obstacles. In conjunction or aspect with the benefics (Moon, Mercury, Jupiter and Venus), Rahu is calmed considerably and its energy is moved upward rather downward.

The Associations of Rahu

- Rahu represents the South West direction. Its colour is smoky blue or smoky black. Its stone is Gomed or Hessonite, and it represents all metals.
- Rahu deals with drugs and poisons. (This creates an element where you can be poisonous to others, but beware of stinging yourself). Rahu also represents diseases - especially smallpox and skin diseases - and cases of suicide, hanging and execution.
- People with a strong Rahu are likely to be tall with a long body.
- Foreigners in all areas - people, countries, and tastes.
- The air element and the sky, Aakash, so it rules all aspects of air-related activities like air travel, including pilots, air travellers and aviation accidents. Rahu loves freedom.
- It rules metaphysical knowledge, witchcraft, inventions, scientists and students of astrology. It also represents deception and disenchantment, politics and political manoeuvring.

Rahu is best placed in the chart alone, and its ideal location is the 3rd, 6th, 10th and 11th houses. If Rahu is also aspected by a benefic like Jupiter, it gives excellent results and protects the person from negative energies. Rahu's most difficult position is the 8th house. It is well placed in Aries, Taurus and Gemini.

Rahu aspects the 5th, 7th, 9th and 12th houses from itself; its aspect is separative in nature and always causes problems. This means that Rahu separates you from the significations of the house it aspects - for example, if Rahu aspects the 7th house, it separates you from your marriage partner, which could lead to divorce if other indications are there.

Rahu is exalted in Taurus and debilitated in Scorpio. Both Maharishi Parashar and Jaimini assign the co-rulership of Aquarius to Rahu.

Rahu Yantra

The Yantra
This is the yantra for Rahu. Yantras are mystical forms that reveal a hidden form or structure and are used in association with other remedial measures. Meditating on the symbol whilst chanting the appropriate mantra is helpful in bringing the energy into your life. See the chapter on Remedial Measures for more information on yantras and mantras.

3

KETU - INTUITION AND ENLIGHTENMENT

Ketu is the tail of the celestial snake. The tail carries all past life karmas and potentials. It has no head, therefore it feels with the heart and reacts instinctively, emotionally and intuitively rather than with the intellectual analysis of conscious thought. Ketu's role in a birth chart is to look beyond the restrictions of the mind and to make the fusion between the consciousness and the subconscious. It opens your world to all sorts of mysteries, and as you focus on your spiritual quest it opens the doors to the vast secret knowledge you carry within yourself.

Ketu is depicted with a star in place of its head, for this is the bright light that shines on an individual when they take the inner path of searching and work to transform their potential from negative to positive. As the seat of the positive kundalini shakti, Ketu allows us to balance the material and the spiritual.

Rejection
Ketu indicates the fear of rejection. Ketu-dominated people are often afraid to experience life fully because of it, and for the same reason are likely to reject others. The fear of Ketu is irrational and instinctive and is usually a test of the ego and pride. Surrendering your inner ego to the higher power, accepting your fear and working on it in a subtle way rather than trying to rationalize it will open the way to its transformation.

The Search for the Impossible
Ketu in the birth chart signifies *moksha* or enlightenment, the state of perfection which the soul seeks to achieve in its journey through various life times. To reach this condition the soul must reject all worldly pleasures and align itself to an altered state of consciousness, where there is no pain, just eternal happiness and peace. This makes Ketu an extremely idealistic planet, seeking a perfection

not possible for most mortals to achieve. Ketu's location gives clues to the area where you are most likely to reject outer realities in a search for happiness. Ketu can be very harsh in its rejections, severely and completely cutting things out from your life. This can create many problems as the idealistic state is only achieved by understanding your inner self.

The Keeper of Past-Life Guilt and Knowledge
Ketu is considered the keeper of the book of past and present karma. It has a tendency to live in the past creating a great emotional feeling and connection to the past life, but often at the cost of not wanting to experience new life. As the body part of the celestial snake, Ketu carries all your emotional baggage and is the receptacle of your karma. Problems arise if you allow the guilt of past deeds to influence your present and you feel your soul carrying this weight.

True Enlightenment
Ketu sees the bigger picture and thinks with the heart but has no ability to discern the small details - yet this is also what gives it the ability to look beyond simply earthly issues. In yoga we try to calm our minds, and in vedic rituals we always bow our heads to the almighty. All these are indications that to really understand ourselves and be in touch with the divine self we have to let go of our intellectual prowess and look beyond the restrictions of the mind. The head or the brain carries within it the karmic restrictions from past lives and the complications put forward by the mind, so to achieve true enlightenment we need to go beyond - in many ways we have to become headless like Ketu.

Wandering Star
Ketu is a wanderer, with no material attachments. It is not interested in worldly goods and will bring disenchantment with material success wherever it is placed. Its aim is for moksha- spiritual realisation.

The Poor Philosopher
Indian *sadhus* or holy men, in bright orange robes and long flowing tresses, who have given up their material life in search of a spiritual one, are Ketu dominated personalities. But even those people with lots of money who are in tune with Ketu will find an odd detachment from the fruits of their labours and will be most happy discussing deep philosophical ideas. Like the sadhus, their material needs are minimal and their love for money lessens.

The Jaimini family who followed the Mimasa School of philosophy are an example of Ketu. Their main concern was the correct interpretations of the vedic rituals and the settling of controversies over the vedic texts. Ketu guides us towards meditation on the nature of creation, towards a true understanding of the universe and the soul's final salvation.

Obscure and Auspicious

Ketu's birth under Abhijit nakshatra (lunar mansion) is considered very auspicious. This is the 28th nakshatra - it is associated with Brahma and connected to the star Vega. Abhijit is no longer used in astrology as it is very far from the ecliptic and appears not to be part of this solar system, yet it was part of the original nakshatra system and harbours a deeper knowledge of the cosmos. Ketu shows both this connection and disconnection, while its obscurity means it is difficult to understand. Ketu is also auspicious in that its impact will be positive - you just need the wisdom to accept it.

Darkness and Revelation

Ketu's connection to the tamassic guna indicates the concealing of the divine light; Ketu can conceal as well as reveal. It can indicate the lack of perception of our own power, hiding our potential until we are prepared to work towards its unveiling. Once we realise this ability the light is effectively turned on.

The Divine Plan

Ketu's divine plan is to cause great impediments. It causes pain. It sets up roadblocks, traffic jams and boulders on life's journey. It wants to change the psyche so we stop looking for answers in just the material world. We learn to leave the excess baggage of past karma behind and work only with the karma of today. The effect of Ketu problems is like going through a ritual of fire and emerging more powerful and more able to deal with whatever life throws at us. Those unwilling to harness the power of Ketu or understand its karmic path experience a challenging existence. Sometimes it is difficult for anyone to stand in the way of Ketu power. In our need to understand and accept our destiny Ketu is doing its work to produce the enlightenment that leads to true wisdom and honour.

The Spiritual Warrior

Ketu acts like Mars. With its sense of adventure and thirst for new experiences, Mars breaks through restrictions and outer crusts with courage, strength, and an indomitable personality. Mars conquers enemies. As the ruler of Aries, the first sign of the zodiac, it represents being born into the realm of materialism. As the ruler of Scorpio it moves from material to spiritual. Both require immense courage, and Ketu brings the courage required to explore our inner world. It conquers the hidden demons that stop our progress on a spiritual level, delving deeply into the mysteries of life so that the outer crust is destroyed and a new direction is achieved. Unknown enemies have to be faced and new experiences lived through, but Ketu breaks through the mental barriers constructed by past lives and present birth to seek a radically different existence on a mystical, spiritual level.

The experience of Ketu is always multi-dimensional. It has the ability to take us through the many different levels of consciousness from the subtle to the gross.

Ketu Dashas are Essentially Spiritual

Ketu rules a dasha lasting 7 years in the planetary life cycle and always has a sting in its tail - one has to be wary of unexpected happenings at the end of one. Ketu dasha is a spiritualizing influence; it can become a search for happiness and enlightenment but we must be careful that we are not searching for the holy grail. Ketu introduces us to unusual characters and personalities during its dasha with the intention of showing the difference between the fake and the real. By the end of this time we realise that the search taken outwardly is usually false and the inner search is that which will bring the real light.

Financial Rewards

Ketu is known as Dhwajah - a flag. When positioned in dignity with a planet it has the capacity to boost its capabilities beyond recognition. For lotteries and windfalls Ketu in conjunction with a benefic can bring rewards beyond your wildest expectations.

The Associations of Ketu

- People with a strong Ketu are usually tall. Its colour is variegated, multi-coloured like a rainbow. It represents lead and its stone is the Cat's Eye
- Ketu is fiery in nature; it signifies accidents or injury especially due to fire.
- It also signifies ascetics, assassinations, clairvoyance, contemplation, desire for knowledge, deep thinking, imprisonment, magical powers, mysticism and poverty.

Mars, Venus and Saturn are Ketu's friends, while the Sun and Moon are its enemies. Jupiter and Mercury are neutral.

Ketu is best placed alone in the chart as it will adversely affect other planets sharing the same sign or house. Ketu located in the 6th, 8th or 12th house increases inner sensitivity. If Rahu is also aspected by a benefic planet like Jupiter at the same time, it gives excellent results and protects the person from negative energies. Ketu's most difficult position is in the 2nd house, while a position in Sagittarius, Capricorn, Aquarius or Pisces intensifies the search for the inner mysteries of life. If Ketu is placed with the Moon in the 12th house it can give psychic powers, or if together with the Sun in the 8th house it can promote contact with highly evolved souls. In the 12th house Ketu gives clairvoyant faculties - it can also cause psychological imbalances if its energy is not properly harnessed. Ketu conjunct Venus can cause sexual problems.

Ketu aspects the 5th, 7th, 9th and 12th houses from itself, is exalted in Scorpio and debilitated in Taurus. Ketu is said to be the co-ruler of Scorpio. It has a 7-year life cycle in the Vimshottari Dasa system.

Ketu Yantra

The Ketu Yantra
This is the yantra for Ketu, shown in Sanskrit. Yantras are mystical forms that reveal a hidden form or structure and are used in association with other remedial measures. Meditating on the symbol whilst chanting the appropriate mantra is helpful in bringing the energy into your life. See the chapter on Remedial Measures for more information on yantras and mantras.

4

The Karmic Axis

The Rahu Ketu axis shows the struggles that each incarnation brings. This axis is complex and hard to fathom; it pulls you apart, churns you up and is responsible for the psychological turmoil involved in finding the meaning of life. As its main impact is on the mind, it deals with the fears and desires deep within your consciousness that have to be brought out and faced. The Rahu Ketu axis links to past life karma and how we come to terms with it: sometimes we live completely in Rahu (present) and other times completely in Ketu (past). This can create havoc if we become polarised. Rahu relates to the experiences in this life, Ketu to the knowledge we bring from the past. Our present experiences are coloured by our past actions, yet this understanding is not obvious to most of us. Rahu Ketu are cut by Vishnu's wheel, the Sudarshan chakra (see the myth), in the same way that we are separated from one part of our nature.

Life should not be a tale of two disconnected halves but of a complete person who flows from past life to the present. Gradually we learn to deal with the crises presented by past life actions and act to stop them occurring again. It is a lack of understanding that creates deep-rooted unhappiness and the karmic purpose is to find answers within to reconcile the outer life with the inner one, the past life with the present. In the beginning the axis creates disharmony, but by becoming aware of the subtler levels of energies at work we gradually acquire the tools to work with the purity of our spirituality and overcome our difficulties.

With Rahu and Ketu there is both darkness and light. They are only visible during an eclipse, as the darkness that surrounds the Sun or Moon during such a time is Rahu Ketu. If Rahu causes the eclipse, then Rahu is visible, if Ketu causes the eclipse, then Ketu is visible. As they are visible so seldom, the nodes can only show their true meaning at rare times. Their true meaning often dawns with sudden insight after years of search and turmoil.

The Rahu Ketu axis reveals our deepest secrets. To access them properly we need to look within and reconcile the polarities we find. Focus on what is hidden to reveal the truth.

Analysing the Axis

This book presents a lot of information for the first time. The Rahu Ketu axis is always couched in enigmatic terms in the ancient classics: while I am staying true to the classical information, I am interpreting it for the student of today, taking the mystical knowledge and trying to make it easier for us to understand.

An analysis of the Rahu Ketu axis has to touch both the physical and the subtle. The deeper you take your journey, the more information you will be privy to. Do not be afraid if you do not understand everything that is revealed as the axis is paradoxical and it takes time comprehend its nuances. Wisdom comes through life experience. This book gives you a source to interpret the information - the more you study it, the more it will reveal to you.

To understand how the soul comes to terms with boundaries created by past lives, we consider the following points in relation to the Rahu Ketu axis:

1.   The house axis. This reveals the area where the conflict between our past life karma and present desires will be fought out.
2.   The signs that rule this house axis represent the strengths or weaknesses we have at our disposal to reconcile these issues.
3.   The nakshatras that rule the axis indicate the subtleties that unveil the spiritual process of Rahu Ketu in the natal chart. For example the 1st / 7th axis is ruled by two planets, but there may be ten differing nakshatras that rule the same area. The nakshatras indicate what is buried deep within the subconscious - the karmic lessons each soul has to experience and overcome.

Step One - The House Axis

The house placement of Rahu Ketu tells us which areas of our lives are likely to be most influenced by karma. For instance, if the axis connects the 4th and 10th houses, the issues will be between inner needs and outer expression, but these issues have not taken root just in this life. Their germination has been in a previous lifetime and the images are being projected into this life. The axis pulls in two directions, so the correct way to deal with it is by bringing it together rather than allowing yourself to be pulled apart. Once you realise both agendas are effectively the same, the axis will start to flow in both directions. You have to learn to give something to the opposite party - love and not rejection for Ketu, give and not take for Rahu.

It is inevitable that either Rahu or Ketu will be negatively placed in your chart. Ketu will show the past life issues you are dealing with, while Rahu indicates your psychological struggles in the here and now.

Past Life Houses
The 4th, 8th and 12th houses are moksha or enlightenment houses. They are also houses where past life issues are dominant. Any connection between Rahu or Ketu and the Ascendant or its ruler creates an extreme focus on past life issues.

Rahu and Ketu are considered good in the upachaya houses, 3rd, 6th, 10th and 11th, where they get progressively better. They are good in the 3rd, better in the 6th, great in the 10th and outstanding in the 11th. Upachaya houses are growth houses; they indicate the ability to improve the quality of life through struggle and difficulty. The nodes placed here show the ability to deal with the shadows of life and learn to overcome the issues that come up.

Rahu in 1st/Ketu in 7th house
This karmic axis is about yourself and your relationships. The pattern of behaviour is connected to selfishness and rejection: Rahu is selfish and Ketu constantly rejects. The flow between Rahu Ketu will be resolved when patterns are changed to one where Rahu learns to be selfless and Ketu can open its heart.

With Rahu placed in the 1st house, you want to personally experience every shade of life. This can make you selfish and self-centred if you do not recognise what you are doing. Rahu in the 1st will make you an intensely materialistic and ambitious person with a desire to achieve wealth and power. As Rahu drives you to impose your personal mark on society you are likely to experience frustration and disenchantment, with feelings of non-achievement despite being successful. The good news is that you have the power to work at a very deep level and if you immerse yourself in humanitarian work you can find deep satisfaction. Your personality is such that no amount of obstacles will have any meaning for you. By striving for a balance between your own and your partner's needs, and by not looking at life from just one view, your heart will slowly open to the great possibilities within yourself. You will be able to achieve your worldly ambitions without sacrificing your spiritual goals and the feeling of emptiness and fear inside will disappear.

Ketu in the 7th house suggests that the chance of finding true happiness in a partnership or marriage is more likely if you understand the subtle lessons it is bringing you. Ketu, seen as the planet of spiritual enlightenment, is not well placed in the house of sensual relationships. As you start to feel dissatisfied with your relationship you may well create situations which hurt your partner, in which case they may decide to leave you and break away from your selfishness. Ketu in the 7th can teach a painful lesson in relationships. When the subtler energies are understood, it is possible to see that two people can function well both as contented individuals and as part of a relationship. With some work, Ketu in the 7th allows you to experience real love.

If the emphasis remains on purely material experiences, it is possible you will always feel dissatisfied with your relationships - without really knowing why. You may be involved in a relationship which is envied by the world, but which doesn't seem good enough to you. In the same way your own success will not satisfy you if you are not doing some internal work. Are you are overdoing things?

Rahu Ketu in this axis can indicate big ambitions that can get you into trouble. Like the seriously rich industrialist who risks his last penny for an even bigger slice of the cake, being over-ambitious can lead to loss.

The best way to connect the 1st/7th house axis is through the heart, by allowing yourself to love another unconditionally. The planets placed in the 4th house in your chart are important as they reflect your heart's desires. Saturn or Mars placed in the 4th, will create mistrust whereas Venus, Jupiter or Moon will allow you to open your 4th house. Yogic exercises, which deal with the anahata or the heart chakra, would also be helpful.

The singer Michael Jackson has this nodal axis, and despite unparalleled success he still has to work hard at relationships. His first marriage was considered a sham and the second has remained in the shadows. Wolfgang Amadeus Mozart, who went against popular opinion to write timeless, beautiful music, and Roseanne Barr, the larger than life American actress also have the 1st/7th axis.

Rahu in 2nd/Ketu in 8th house

The 2nd is the house of speech, wealth, early childhood, insight and potential, whereas the 8th is the house of longevity, death, transformation and the secret knowledge of the past. This karmic axis is considered one of the most difficult as its connection with the positive and negative potential of the individual means there is less free will here. People born with this nodal axis may have a tendency towards financial dependence on others or feel that the world owes them a living. This attitude arises from Rahu's link with the past life potential in the 2nd house. Rahu feels that it should get merit for all its past actions and is anxious to externalise everything for its own profit.

Rahu in the 2nd makes a powerful orator. It can give a strong, mysterious and sometimes harsh voice which can have a hypnotic effect on an audience. Speaking must be subject to awareness and control in normal conversation as it could alienate others. The 2nd house also deals with eating and what we take into our bodies, so Rahu can lead you towards eating and drinking the wrong kind of food and drink. Having said all this, Rahu in the 2nd gives a tremendous insight into life.

The 2nd/8th house axis is linked to the wealth of others. Regardless of how well you are doing in life, there may always be an underlying feeling that others are not sharing their wealth with you fairly: this could lead to the extreme of litigation to get what you feel you are owed. This is not necessarily material wealth; it could also indicate the intellectual heritage of your family. You need to release yourself from such past life karma and learn to stand alone. This axis also has a lot to say about the happiness in your relationships as it concerns the wealth of your partner and their family too; the 2nd house is concerned with your mode of communicating and the 8th is that of your partner's. Remember that the nodes have the sting of the serpent, so beware of hurtful words. When this axis is in a fiery mood and feeling destructive, learn the lesson of containing your harsh words, try and connect with the other's family needs and be up front about financial affairs. When you start giving in your relationships the Rahu Ketu axis will cease to create turmoil.

The spiritual meaning of this axis links the intuition of the 2nd house with the occult mysteries of the 8th. The immense possibilities for divine insight and knowledge are so profound that others may be in awe of you. Ketu in the 8th allows you to look deeply into the world of psychic ability and knowledge from the past, but its energy is difficult to fathom; whilst it is a good placement for spiritual attainment, you may feel frustrated at your apparent inability to communicate this knowledge. There is an underlying fear of expressing what you know in case its complexity is misunderstood. The 2nd/8th axis deals with this struggle, and some might find it easier to deny this knowledge and live life at a more shallow level.

Martin Luther King had Rahu in the 2nd house, as did the famous 12th century Arab astrologer Al Biruni. Heavyweight boxer and legend Mohammed Ali was renowned for his pre-fight banter, and Napoleon Bonaparte was a powerful orator.

Rahu in 3rd/Ketu in 9th house

The 3rd/9th house axis links the lower mind to the higher mind, practical instincts to idealistic desires, and personal efforts to paternal influences. This axis is most noticeable when you do not allow others - especially your father - to control your actions. You seek and follow your own counsel rather than following existing religions or philosophies.

With Rahu in the 3rd, the relationship with your father may be very difficult. This may either be through actual separation and a feeling of rejection, or the need to avoid becoming a conduit for his desires and ambitions. He may project his personality so strongly on your psyche that you end up cutting all ties with him and rebuffing his parental guidance. In Vedic philosophy your father is considered to be your karma. The soul chooses its parents before birth, so it is the actions from a past life that decide what kind of parent you are going to have. A personality clash can only be resolved through having the self-confidence to acknowledge your parent's karmic connection as a guide. If you are comfortable with this axis you may follow your father in his profession, but there will always be an underlying feeling that you have not fulfilled your potential. This is one of the best positions for Rahu as it gives ambition, courage and a sense of adventure. You are intellectually restless and need interesting and stimulating work, but doing too much of your own thing means other people can often take second place. Forming relationships can be difficult. The main problem of this axis is the unwillingness to listen to advice, and the fear of losing your individuality if you do. Realise that listening to others does not make you a weak person; Rahu in the 3rd house is all-powerful, so you can let go of this particular fear. Many people with this axis manage to carve their own niche in life although they began by being an ideal son or daughter to their father, working out the parental wishes.

Ketu in the 9th house gives a strong need to follow a path to enlightenment through philosophies and teachings that are not of your own culture. You have an unconventional approach to religion and Ketu here will bring you a guru who has a great insight into spiritual matters. Be careful to avoid any cult where the guru is not ethical or straightforward.

Madonna, Mia Farrow and Brigitte Bardot, all strong women in their own way, have this nodal axis.

Rahu in 4th/Ketu in 10th house
The 4th house symbolises karma from your past lives and the 10th house indicates the karma of your future. This is a powerful karmic position, but as Rahu naturally deals with the future and Ketu with the past, the two energies are mixed up. The confusion tells you that work started in the past is not complete and there are still problems to be sorted out. The karma of work was very important in a past life which can mean that you now either have a deep-rooted fear of being out in the world or ruthlessly pursue career goals without bothering about others.

If it is the latter you must try to understand your need now for a simpler life and not let work rule you. You can do this by becoming more involved in your home environment. The 4th -10th axis also relates to the home life in that the 4th is your home and your mother and the 10th is your partner's mother. The wishes or even the interference of your partner's mother can be a problem; unhappiness in the home can create conflict in other areas of life so you need to work at any deep sense of dissatisfaction you feel within yourself.

The 4th house is also connected with inner feelings, and Rahu placed here can lead to intense secrecy and keeping a part of the personality hidden. When you meet people with this axis, you may find them hard to understand - however much they project open friendliness, you know they are keeping a part of themselves private. Greta Garbo made privacy an art form, disappearing to live in complete isolation after an extremely successful acting career. Mata Hari, the famous female spy of the 1st World War, is another example of this axis. And finally U.S. President John F. Kennedy, whose outer persona masked a darker private life, shared this placement. If your inner world seems full of darkness, understand that as you look into the dark your eyes will become accustomed to it and the fear within will slowly disappear. Do not be afraid of what the future has in store for you. Difficulties in expressing yourself in the outer world are symptomatic of being stuck in the immediate past or a past life where you had not sorted out personal issues.

Ketu in the 10th house can be afraid to express its full potential, however Ketu is considered very well placed here. It is important to put the emphasis more on the 10th house issues and avoid concentrating on those at the other end of the axis. Any fear of rejection in the outer world can be overcome by choosing a career which is alternative, unconventional and unusual. Many successful astrologers are born with this combination. Ketu in the 10th gives past life knowledge to operate in the present, so professions like archaeology, antiques, history, research, spiritualism and philosophy can be ideal expressions of this axis. There are also a number of successful actors who are born with this axis as Ketu in the 10th attracts them to playing unusual roles where they can hide their inner personalities by acting out different personas. Tom Hanks, Kevin Costner, Greta Garbo and Robbie Coltrane are among them. Judy Garland, is also illustrative of this axis. She had a very successful 10th house career, but Rahu's position in the 4th exacerbated her fears, which she then tried to conquer through drugs and alcohol. In contrast Tom Hanks, with his portrayal of unusual characters such as Forrest Gump, illustrates the positive and multi-coloured potential of Ketu in the 10th house.

Rahu in 5th/Ketu in 11th house
The karmic axis of the 5th and 11th house is about creativity and the fruits of your life, both material and spiritual. This creativity can be expressed through children, ideas, higher and abstract thinking. Children become very important for you but the axis can also refer in an abstract sense to the fruits of your creativity. The 5th/11th houses can sometimes bring problems with having children or a fear of losing them. You must avoid being too protective or possessive and try to allow them the freedom to develop their own personalities. Lessons learnt from your children will be important; their partnerships and relationships will have a major impact on you.

On a creative level you can be very fertile. Rahu will make you ambitious to achieve the highest form of creativity but you may not necessarily be interested in material results. Many writers, poets and artists have Rahu in the 5th house; Picasso is a prime example. As Rahu deals with shadows, writers who focus on the shadowy world of mystery and crime are especially strongly represented here. This axis will forever be bringing you to the creative areas of your life but you must pay attention to the practicalities. An over-indulgence in creativity can create difficulties in being with others, or you may be a creative genius with no idea how to handle finances. Finding your true identity through creativity is the most important lesson. The 5th house is also the house of entertainment; Oprah Winfrey, Woody Allen, Ernest Hemingway, Elizabeth Taylor and Whitney Houston have this axis.

The 11th is connected with gains. As Ketu focuses your mind to higher principles it is not primarily interested in work on a materialistic level, so there can be many financial dilemmas. Yet Ketu's mystical side can suddenly bring untold financial gains and the ability to make lots of money. What often happens however is that either the money is given up voluntarily through philanthropic activity or no pleasure is gained at all from financial success. But if you are looking for gains on a spiritualistic level, it can bring them forth in immense quantities.

Rahu in 6th/Ketu in 12th house
This axis links the 6th house (service, obstacles, enemies and disease) to the 12th (loss, imprisonment, sexual pleasures, clairvoyance and moksha). It is a strong position for the Rahu Ketu axis. Rahu will remove all obstacles in your path and can help slay your inner demons, while Ketu naturally wants to move towards enlightenment. Your enemies will be strong, but you will be able to handle and destroy them.

Many people with this axis have strong and unknown enemies, who could possibly bring them down. Indira Gandhi, the powerful Indian Prime Minister had the ability to control her detractors but she was always aware of secret enemies and plots. Bill Gates, the founder of Microsoft, is battling with the U.S. government to keep his empire intact. Saddam Hussein took on the world in the Gulf War and still survived against all odds.

Rahu in the 6th house indicates people who are very good in competitive situations but need to learn how to assess others. Are they friends or foes? Issues connected with your sexual pleasures and needs (either you are afraid to enjoy sex or you may over-indulge) are likely. When you are younger you may experience obstacles regarding work, disease or enemies, but you will have more than average ability to deal with this. (Mysterious illnesses which are hard to diagnose and which disappear suddenly are typical). After dealing with mundane problems in the early part of your life you can move towards controlling your personal desires through meditation and yoga. Once you reach that stage, the natural progression will be moving towards moksha or spiritual realisation.

Ketu as the moksha karaka is in its own house and so provides a powerful instrument for spiritual fulfilment and higher understanding. You are introspective and probably need to be alone a great deal; Ketu in the 12th house represents knowledge gained as part of your karma from the chain of lives and deaths which will be useful to you in finding final salvation.

Rahu in 7th/Ketu in 1st house

The 1st/7th axis is again of self and relationships, but this axis will be different to having Rahu in the 1st and Ketu in the 7th. This time Rahu's position in the 7th house indicates that although you are in some ways a loner, relationships will dominate your life and you need to experience them in every hue. This can lead to a promiscuous personality but also a dissatisfied one regardless of how many relationships you experience. It is important here to recognise the inner dilemma: fulfilment will not be gained by creating yet another relationship, but by trying to work out the present one and acknowledging that there are always two sides to every story.

Ketu in the 1st house indicates a karmic past life connection. You may be carrying over guilt from previous lives that is now blocking you on a psychological level and causing you to blame yourself for others' actions, and you have to learn to let that go. These are past life issues, and bringing them into this life will not give any answers. Take care not to see yourself from a completely negative point of view. Often, in compensation, identity and fulfilment is expressed wholly through partnerships. You may have come into contact at an early age with people whose negative behaviour towards you had a lasting impact. Ketu in the 1st gives an ability to hold on to things, and you still feel and remember past events which you should let go. You really need to have an emotional clear out every so often otherwise you may find yourself suffering physically or psychologically.

Jackie Kennedy, John Kennedy's widow, has this axis. She had major lessons to learn from her relationships - first with John F. Kennedy, and then through her marriage to the Greek millionaire Aristotle Onassis. The 'Superman' actor Christopher Reeve, who has Ketu exactly conjunct his Ascendant, has powerful karmic issues to deal with in this life. Through his debilitating accident, his wife has become a strong support. Clint Eastwood has had multiple marriages/ relationships and Ketu in the 1st has given him an unusual personality and screen persona. Ketu acts like Mars and Clint Eastwood's films have always been noted for both their violence and action.

Rahu in 8th/Ketu in 2nd house

This axis is a difficult one. Rahu and Ketu are debilitated in Scorpio and Taurus; the 8th is the natural house for Scorpio and the 2nd is the natural house for Taurus. In this the underworld becomes activated and our latent power is located as the kundalini rests dormant here. Both the 2nd and the 8th houses have a powerful connection with hidden potential - both negative and positive. The 8th is a multi-layered house dealing with the hidden areas of life, and it is difficult to gauge what subtle energies may be experienced here. Rahu, which makes little distinction between good and bad, has the thirst to experience everything including the urge to activate the kundalini - but are you ready for it? Do you have a good teacher who can help you bring forth these powerful energies? In this arena of transformation and change you need knowledge and wisdom to deal with these energies successfully. The urge to explore the dark reaches of society and dive into the still waters of human knowledge is very strong, and must be properly harnessed or it could lead to difficulties with crime, drugs or power games; the positive use of it brings higher wisdom. People with this placement of Rahu Ketu can become great scientists, researchers, astrologers, and archaeologists.

Ketu in the 2nd house can symbolize a disconnection with your childhood. There may have been a feeling of rejection or loneliness at school that makes you feel a misfit - you may not share society's expected need to be materialistic and family loving. The 2nd house link to speech may produce people with speech defects or those who talk in a straightforward no-frills way but end up alienating others. Alternatively the outward speech may be sweet, but is a mask for resentment and anger within.

The deep significance of the 8th house Rahu is difficult to handle at a young age and these people may later become involved in far-distance travel, moving to experiment with the secrets of the world. It is a difficult journey.

There is alienation and unhappiness yet if one truly understands this axis it can become the house of deep natural wisdom and incisive insight. This psychic ability can be frightening but at the same time if properly handled it can give visions of both the future and the past. My main advice to those having this axis is to practice yoga from a young age. It has to be accepted that these people are likely to be either unwilling or unable to fulfil what the world demands of them as their karmic path is linked to the deeper resources of nature. They can look beyond the ordinary. Not all souls are intended to live within the social norms.

The 8th-2nd axis has a similar influence on relationships to its counterpart the 2nd-8th, with the same family issues: in-laws that your partner does not like will be asking for attention and there can be many sarcastic and biting words exchanged. In turn Ketu in the 2nd can make you verbally reject your partner's family. Rahu in the 8th shows your partner's focus or obsession with his family and Ketu in the 2nd shows your own difficulties with them. You have to be very careful not only to be disciplined about each other's money but to learn to be more accepting of your partner's family.

One of the most important aspects of this axis is to ensure that you have a sattvic lifesyle: pure vegetarian, non-spicy food, lots of water and as little alcohol and drugs as possible. Visual abstinence means avoiding noisy places, television and loud music as all these disturb your peace of mind. There is an aspect in yoga called *pratyahara* - a discipline which teaches you to withdraw from the senses and is the first stage in concentrating the mind. Both Alexander Graham Bell and Albert Einstein used the 8th house Rahu energies to move into previously undiscovered areas. They used this energy positively through research and innovation, leading them to make discoveries that changed the life of countless others. Richard Nixon perhaps expressed the more negative side of this axis through the political manipulation of Watergate; a scandal that forced him to resign from the office of President of the United States.

Rahu in 9th/Ketu in 3rd house

The 9th/3rd house axis is the link between the higher to the lower mind. The positions are reversed to that of the 3rd/9th axis for here Rahu is in the house of the dharmic path. Now Rahu has the need to experience gurus and issues of higher knowledge, while Ketu is linked to life's practical issues including personal efforts, ambitions and desires. By nature Ketu is connected to the abstract mind and usually wants to give up material issues, so here it will manifest itself in life in an abstract, unusual and eccentric way. Material ties will still not bind it, and its opposite force (Rahu) will want to impress others with its knowledge and power. This is usually a position seen in the charts of people who present a religion or philosophy in a new and innovative way. On the negative side this axis could bring manipulation and self-righteousness, but Rahu in the 9th gives the potential to become a great teacher.

Rahu is said to bring fame in the 9th house. Although traditional astrologers have not favoured Rahu in the 9th as a good position, many modern astrologers feel that Rahu in the house of good luck can bring immense rewards, especially if the 9th house ruler is well placed. Classical astrologers did not like Rahu in the 9th as it gave a fondness for foreign cultures, but in the multicultural society of the modern world this is no longer a negative situation. Ketu in the 3rd house is well placed too, and the axis has great potential once you go beyond its initial issues of father and siblings.

Ketu in the 3rd house also brings an urge to present ideas to others in a way that fascinates and influences those around them. Politicians often have this placement including both Tony Blair and Bill Clinton. The paternal relationship can be difficult. There may be separation from the father or a life under the control of a dominating father. It is not an easy relationship, as paternal issues will dominate your life regardless of whether you are close to your father or not. You may worry about not being able to live up to his high expectations. There is also a strong past life contact with your siblings. At times you may feel that on some level you owe them something and their needs are not allowing you to progress. Usually there is a past life debt being repaid to them in this life. If you do not have any brothers or sisters, the connection may be with a close friend or someone in your peer group.

Other examples of this axis include: Richard Branson who has had a great influence in Britain through his 'Virgin' empire; Michael Douglas who achieved immense fame following in his father's film career, and Charlie Chaplin whose fame has lasted beyond his lifetime.

Rahu in 10th/Ketu in 4th house

As the node concerning your future, Rahu is well placed in the 10th, the house where you lay down your future karma. You will live your life on a large canvas and will feel frustrated if not expressing yourself properly. There is a link between your past life karma and your present life actions. Emotional issues may be hard to cope with and a difficult relationship with your mother and your home is possible. Your mother may be holding on to you through feelings of guilt, and your life is very tied to maternal issues. The feeling of loneliness and disenchantment forces you to live your life in the outer world where you have the capacity to sway the consciousness of many people, and others see only the successful side of your nature.

You have a strong sense of destiny and a belief that you must make a name for yourself. Women especially have a strong attachment to their home, but also the drive to give up that comfort and lead life in the public arena. Many world leaders and personalities are born with this configuration. In fact Rahu in the 10th can give such super-charged ambition that no amount of outward success can ever satisfy it. Your search is really for happiness through outer success but you may find this whole issue difficult if there is an unresolved situation with your mother. It is important to look into your heart and come to terms with your inner emptiness, then break the pattern of rejection and move towards unconditional love.

Ketu, the node of the past, is very strong in the 4th house of past life. The relationship with the mother is considered a past life one, the soul choosing the parents to complete the karmic equation. Once you are born you cannot change this relationship but you can improve its quality, by reconciling the fact that it is karmic there are lessons for both if it is enacted fully. There is a possibility that you may either reject your mother or feel rejected by her so it is important to discuss this aspect. The obvious path is to move away from the maternal relationship and block your mind to it, but the pain so caused becomes projected on your ambitions and outer personality. This is a pattern you need to break.

Princess Diana's relationship with her mother and the rejection she felt from her parents' divorce created the unhappiness within her, yet Rahu in the 10th made her a global personality. Agatha Christie also had a troubled home life, yet was famous for her writings.

Rahu in 11th/Ketu in 5th house
The 11th/5th axis is one of the best for Rahu Ketu, promising much material success. Rahu in the 11th will bring financial rewards and respect from others, but you may remain dissatisfied with your personal achievements unless you carry them out in your own individual way. You will have to learn to be a true 'New Ager', more of a free spirit. You need to leave behind the philosophy of 'I - Me' and learn to interact with others.

Rahu in the 11th is said to give everlasting fame - you can use your talents to make money and will be remembered for a long time even after your death. The belief is that Rahu placed here will always give its disciples immense wealth; meditation on the meaning of the placement may help if you find this energy difficult. When you start to trust your abilities and stop worrying about the finances the situation will improve dramatically.

Ketu in the 5th links you with abstract knowledge and a real and deep understanding of life. Here the intellect will be powerful, with the ability to positively express new ideas and past life knowledge in an innovative form. The feeling of past life karma is very strong as the 5th house shows how you externalise your past lives into creative activity in this lifetime. You will be driven to find a way to make all the achievements of your past lives work for you this time. However, Ketu in the house of children and creative enterprises can cause other problems. It will always be difficult to find your true creativity until you start using it for the good of others. As the tail of the serpent, Ketu is a headless - the 5th house deals with intellect so sometimes Ketu's placement here leads to people pretending to be dumb or stupid. There is a possibility that very intelligent people will deliberately ignore their abilities and take on careers where they do not use they mind as they do not feel that they are bright. Once they do start using their mind however, they can be very successful in intellectual pursuits as, for example, writers or advisors. Ketu in the 5th can bring old ideas and express them in a creative new way. President George W. Bush is a classic example of Ketu in the 5th - public perception fuelled by the media leads us to think he is not particularly intelligent, whereas his birth chart suggests otherwise.

There are many famous people with this axis: Arthur Ashe, Bjorn Borg, Coco Chanel, Cheiro, James Dean, Stephen King, Bruce Lee and Osho. These people all remained famous long after the events that first brought them renown. Arthur Ashe was the first black tennis champion of Wimbledon, and Bjorn Borg won Wimbledon five times. Coco Chanel was the fashion designer whose name lives on, and actor James Dean made just three films before his early death yet his fame is undiminished.

Rahu in 12th/Ketu in 6th house

The 12th /6th axis represents loss, endings, expenses, sexual pleasures and enlightenment. On one level the 12th house reflects your hidden indulgences through extravagance or sexual activities but alternatively it represents the highest achievement that the soul can experience: enlightenment and the breaking away from the cycles of life and death.

Rahu will have to experience this house in all its shades. You could have a secret sexual life with a great need to enjoy such pleasures to a negative extreme, but this indulgence will not find happiness. It is important to understand that just as spending a lot of money can give a momentary thrill, sexual orgasm only leads to momentary pleasure. There is an inherent dissatisfaction connected with this axis until you control the power of Rahu and understand the positive energies of the 12th house, which deal with accepting the cycles of life and death. For those already seeking higher consciousness, the materialistic high achiever Rahu creates a desire for the highest level of karmic salvation. A sudden transformation takes place making you aware of the spiritual path you need to follow. Your urge to explore unknown lands and achieve true nirvana is very strong.

Ketu can cause great unhappiness in the pursuit of daily life, and if you are not following a spiritual path this placement could be very difficult. Ketu in the 6th rejects the traditional work ethic, often seeking unusual occupations and it can create powerful enemies, real or imagined. Sudden illnesses may block the path of material success and Rahu's position in the 12th may cause you to spend more than you earn.

One amazing aspect of this axis is the number of famous film stars that have it in their charts. The 12th house association with clairvoyance and psychic energy can be transformed into the filmworld of fantasy and illusion, and Rahu's strong sensual energy marks the attraction of legendary stars like Marilyn Monroe, Cher, Josephine Baker, Liberace, Harrison Ford, Cary Grant, Peter Sellers, and Dustin Hoffman. It may also be that Ketu in the 6th house of competition encourages a successful film star to succeed against great odds. Very few actors are handed their stardom on a plate; they have to struggle to achieve the impossible - a very Ketu aspiration. This is the strength of Ketu in the 6th, it gives the ability to conquer the greatest obstacles and in some way find the hidden fruit of success within a material world.

5

RAHU KETU THROUGH THE SIGNS

Rahu Ketu are your own personal demons, the fears and complexes that need to be overcome to gain happiness and peace of mind. The way they will affect your life is dictated by the signs in which they are placed. Will this intensify their impact or not? Do the dispositors of the sign understand how to link the axis together or will your life always be pulled between spiritual and material desires? The lesson of Rahu Ketu is to suppress the enemy within and bring out the friend; the polarity inherent in this axis is fought in your sub-conscious and the thoughts arising from it influence your actions in daily life.

As Rahu Ketu are shadow planets they take on the colour and characteristics of the signs and planets that rule them. While the houses indicate the areas of life that dominate, the signs and their rulers give information on how to work with the axis. For example, the 2nd/8th house axis is considered difficult, but if your 2nd house is Taurus and 8th is Scorpio then Rahu Ketu are placed in their exaltation signs. Furthermore if Mars (the ruler of Scorpio) is placed in Capricorn and Venus (the ruler of Taurus) is in Libra, Mars will be in its exaltation sign and Venus will be in its own sign too. Also in this arrangement Venus is placed in a 10th house from Mars and Mars is placed in a 4th from Venus - a good mutual position. This apparently difficult axis then becomes very positive. What may intially seem to be a difficulty in your chart can change due to the strength of the planets - then you are able to access the positive aspects of the axis.

Rahu in Aries/Ketu in Libra
Aries conveys newness and a sense of adventure, of moving into unexplored territory. Rahu in Aries wants to experience this new cycle of birth intensely. The focus here is on individuality and power and as both Rahu and Mars are

fearless, there is no recognition of boundaries or restrictions. You are likely to be competitive, adventurous, individualistic, brave, ambitious, always looking for new thrills and excitement. Mars and Rahu do not have a particularly good relationship because the power of Mars is physical while Rahu is psychological. so Rahu in an Aries personality can burn out quickly if its energy is not disciplined. It is naturally a free spirit, enjoying a life without commitments or responsibility. If you have this position you have so much power in your hands that it is necessary to control this force and use it wisely to bring out the best in yourself. Remember you are often your own worst enemy - fear of personal failure can make you selfish, stubborn and egotistical as you focus more and more on your personal agenda. Become more responsible for your own actions and other situations will fall into place.

People with Ketu in Libra search for their spirituality through relationships. They will reject many partners while searching for the perfect mate, often focusing too much on spirituality and forgetting the Libran principal of balancing the opposites: the spiritual and the material, themselves and others, the outer world in the inner. The relationships that last are likely to be unconventional and intangible as Ketu in Libra makes your judgements abstract and hard for others to understand.

Rahu in Aries will try to dominate and emphasise the personal agenda, then Ketu in Libra will pull the other way to find spirituality through partnerships - and then reject them. On one hand you will be extremely strong, on the other you give up your strength and allow your partner to dictate. You may believe you are paying a karmic debt to this other person (who may be your partner, father or child, depending on the appropriate house axis). But both are unhappy situations, as you will be working from only one part of the axis or the other.

Past life issues: Ketu in Libra will indicate past life issues connected with relationships. This focus on partnership was once so strong that it is either blocked now through rejection of others or partners are met who bring the same past life karma you are working out.

Lessons of the Aries/Libra axis: reconciling the opposites is the important issue. There has to be a connection between others and yourself. Rahu in Aries becomes obsessed with stamping its authority on the world; there are no boundaries and restrictions too great for it to surmount. Ketu in Libra feels Rahu's search for new worlds as a personal rejection. Rahu in Aries needs to take its focus away from the individual, while Ketu in Libra has to be prepared to give the relationship a chance to develop. You have to break the opposite patterns of rejection and personal fulfilment and connect the two together.

Mars is neutral to Venus so their relationship with each other will depend on how they are placed in your chart. Physical actions are not paramount; you also have to seek psychological answers.

Rahu in Taurus/Ketu in Scorpio
Taurus represents creative potential - sex, procreation, and material desire. Rahu and Venus are friends and Rahu is exalted in Taurus. Its immense ambition is checked by Taurean practicalities so it becomes disciplined as it works towards success; the Venus influences allow it to express its desires properly. This position gives immense potential as there is a natural ability to understand the Rahu ambition and control its phenomenal power to create something beautiful. This could mean success in areas like the arts, media, and entertainment (see Steven Spielberg's chart later in the book). Provided you do not ignore your material responsibilities, Rahu in Taurus gives you the tools to be happy within your given circumstances.

Ketu in Scorpio is exalted too. Ketu acts like Mars, the ruler of Scorpio. This is a complex and difficult sign but Ketu understands these complexities as it is also involved in the deep mysteries of life. You will be interested in researching the subtle energies of nature and hidden knowledge. Ketu is without ego and Scorpio learns to break from individual identification towards the final lonely path of spiritual fulfilment. The strength of Mars and Venus will decide which of the nodes dominate in your life. It will indicate whether the attraction of Rahu materialism is stronger than Ketu spiritualism. If Mars and Venus are not well placed in respect of each other, it can create turmoil and disconnection of the duality. However if they are in harmony with each other, you will find the strong polarities working well, producing an individual who is at peace with both their material and spiritual self.

Past life Issues: Ketu in Scorpio indicates a past life where the search for the mystical power of nature dominated. The hidden power of kundalini lies dormant in Scorpio, so this power was once explored and its experiences still stored in the psyche. Rahu in Taurus is essentially practical, using past life experiences for practical purposes.

Lessons of Taurus/Scorpio axis: This can either be the easiest axis to work or the most difficult one. As both Rahu and Ketu are exalted, it is easy for the individual to live in either one of the two energies - you can be exploring a purely materialistic path or a deeply spiritual one, and here lies the dilemma. The soul is pulled in two strong directions as it feels that one path is disconnected from the other. Those with Taurus/Scorpio axis must remember that the path of material satisfaction is as much a part of the soul's purpose as is the spiritual one. When you become comfortable with both sides of your nature the duality of the axis becomes reconciled.

Rahu in Gemini/Ketu in Sagittarius

Rahu and Ketu are well placed in Gemini and Sagittarius respectively. Mercury rules Gemini, and Rahu - the thinking head of the celestial snake - finds a conduit for its intellectual expression here. It enjoys the analytical nature of Gemini and its search to find answers to the purpose of the soul. Being of a dual nature Gemini can intellectualise and be business-like at the same time, so it becomes a thinker and a planner, a good researcher with a political bent of mind. But be careful not to allow the negative manipulative powers of Rahu to dominate your intellect for this position can create a real sense of dissatisfaction with the current state of affairs in your life - whatever they may be. Let go of the fear of failing intellectually and stop re-examining yourself. Be realistic. If you can change things then do so, otherwise learn to accept them. This will help towards your personal happiness.

Sagittarius represents the stage in the cosmic cycle where the animal turns into human, striving to control its lower impulses so that the soul can move ahead on its final journey. Sagittarius is a Kshatriya, a warrior. Ketu is also a spiritual warrior so it is in harmony with this Sagittarian impulse. Ketu takes on Jupiter's mantle of the spiritual teacher acquiring the ability to teach in a deeply mystical way but although Ketu the demon and Jupiter the divine teacher do not have a good relationship with each other, Ketu benefits immensely from its placement in Sagittarius. Your own need for knowledge leads you to find a teacher who will guide you towards your true self, even though Ketu keeps making you renounce your teachers, your native religion, and the sources of your knowledge.

Past Life Issues: The past life connection of Ketu in Sagittarius is with divine teaching. The past life slowly changed the direction of your desires from outer to inner. Your psyche remains a fund of passive knowledge, which only becomes available in this life once you learn to use this knowledge unconditionally.

Lessons of Gemini/Sagittarius axis: As both the shadow planets are strong in this axis, the strength of their dispositors will need to be judged carefully. Mercury is neutral towards Jupiter but Jupiter treats Mercury as an enemy. Rahu in Gemini is comfortable with the past life issues it brings into this life but Ketu in Sagittarius will not be happy to share. Their rulers have a difficult agenda. According to the myth of Tara, Mercury is the stepchild of Jupiter, so the trust between the two planets has to be developed; it does not come naturally.

The past life spirituality that Ketu in Sagittarius suggests needs expression through the Gemini intellect. If it is not projected properly Ketu will not be ready to pass on its knowledge to Rahu in Gemini; both the polarities have to give a little. Once Rahu realises the pride it has about its knowledge is only a reflection of what was gathered in previous lives, and Ketu sees that past life knowledge is not enough unless it finds a conduit to express it in the current life, the two energies become fused and the connection from the past to the present is established.

Rahu in Cancer/Ketu in Capricorn

Cancer represents the soul learning to live in a material realm and Capricorn is the soul in a material realm learning to move towards its spiritual path. Rahu should be comfortable with the material expression of Cancer and Ketu with the spiritual expression of Capricorn, but both are uncomfortable with other parts of the Cancer/Capricorn axis. Cancer is ruled by the emotional Moon and Rahu prefers to work on the intellectual realm so it feels uncomfortable here. Many classical astrologers feel that Rahu is good in Cancer, but in my opinion this is a difficult position. Rahu in Cancer can create a fear of emotion, always trying to put a rational slant on your feelings. The more you do that, the greater the turmoil you create.

Ketu, the spiritual warrior who wants nothing more than to disconnect with the world, is in Capricorn: the sign obsessed with facing its karma. Saturn rules Capricorn and Saturn believes in facing up to reality, but Ketu pulls away from these restrictions, fearing attachments and rejecting discipline and hard work.

Past Life Issues: Ketu in Capricorn shows a past life where karmic debts were repaid and the work ethic was paramount as the soul was learning to break away from its practical ambitions. Rahu in Cancer suggests a reflection of the past life in a material realm again. This leads to a confusion of the soul's true purpose. It appears at first that this is a regression back to materialism.

Lessons of Cancer/Capricorn axis: This axis can create great stress if it becomes too focused on Ketu. Rahu in Cancer wants emotional happiness yet fears its consequences, while Ketu in Capricorn believes in self-denial. For this axis to work well, you have to stop denying your need for love and happiness. The realisation that past and present lives are intertwined and there are no clear cut demarcation lines between them, makes this axis easier to understand.

The Moon and Saturn have a complex relationship with each other. The Moon is emotional and Saturn rigid, hence Rahu becomes extremely unstable in its attitude while Ketu becomes fundamentalist and unyielding. This axis tends to be focused on Ketu issues as Saturn does not allow you to forget the lessons of austerity, duty and renunciation that were learnt in past lives. For personal growth and development it is necessary at times to just let go.

Rahu in Leo/Ketu in Aquarius

Leo allows the inner being to express itself in the material world and Rahu embraces this materialism. Leo is naturally connected to Rahu which is said to be borne on a lioness. With Rahu representing psychological power and Leo representing physical prowess, together they can be a powerful combination. Leo is a fiery sign and Rahu's element is air so they can fan each other's qualities and become uncontrollable. Alternatively Rahu can sometimes extinguish Leo's brightness and idealism and cause depression. As Leo's ruler, the Sun is said to be eclipsed by Rahu, yet at the same time Rahu is only visible at the time of an eclipse. Thus in Leo it has the ability to come out of the shadows and appear for what it is. This makes it a powerful placement for Rahu, which will project its personality while darkening the glory of Leo's ruler.

Ketu in Aquarius is ruled by Saturn. Aquarius is an air sign and Ketu's element is fire, so it represents the same combination of fire and air as before. Aquarius is the sign where individuality can be discarded completely and Ketu is comfortable with this. Saturn is still concerned with reality and focusing on karma but this is easier than in Capricorn. Ketu in Aquarius is very idealistic but there is a danger of fundamentalism as Saturn can become very rigid in its views.

The relationship of the Sun and Saturn is a difficult one because Saturn is the rejected son of the Sun god. The Sun stands for individual glory and Saturn for democratic principles; the conflict will be reflected in this axis. Ketu in Aquarius and Rahu in Leo will always be fighting for supremacy, but the true understanding of this axis is that one can work for democratic principles while retaining an individual personality. There may always be a vulnerability over expressing individuality but the conflict is resolved by being comfortable with your personality.

Past Life Issues: Ketu in Aquarius represents a past life spent in service to others. There was a disconnection with self and a focus on selflessness; living as a sadhu or wanderer in a past life was mainly to gain knowledge and work for others. The result is that you may now find yourself feeling guilty of your personal needs.

Lessons of Leo/Aquarius axis: Problems arise over the lack of personal confidence that Ketu in Aquarius brings into this life and which Rahu in Leo now struggles to overcome. Neither Saturn nor Ketu have much love for personal glory but Rahu in Leo has to fulfil its spiritual task to bring out the hidden personality. If the axis is disconnected, there is an immense feeling of guilt over pursuing personal gains and fame. Rahu in Leo will become depressed and dejected if its individuality is not allowed to shine so it is important to accept this need. Similarly Ketu in Aquarius will need to express its democratic principles and public service path so the axis connects when you use your personality to work for others as well as yourself.

Rahu in Virgo/Ketu in Pisces

Virgo fulfils the divine plan through actively participating in the material world. This can leave a deep dissatisfaction within as the soul feels enclosed in matter. As Rahu's role is essentially material though with spiritual awareness as a result, it is very well placed in Virgo. Yet Rahu also emphasises the discontentment in this purely material task. The more successful one becomes, the greater the feeling of emptiness within. The Rahu lesson is that consciousness has to attune itself to fulfilling its material role as an act of service for future karma. In Virgo, Rahu's role is connected to doing a job well in order to open the gateway for further spiritual success in succeeding lifetimes.

Ketu in Pisces is also very well placed. It is the moksha planet, in the sign of moksha. But from a purely practical point of view, this can be a position of unrealistic expectation. Ketu in Pisces is searching for Utopia. The individual can be so idealistic and spiritual that they find it difficult to live in the world of matter. They tend to look at the world through rose-tinted glasses, and feel disappointed when hardly anything or anyone lives up to their dream. While being a perfect position for those on a divine path, Ketu in Pisces can create problems in the real world.

Past Life Issues: Ketu in Pisces feels it is a reflection of the absolute. The past life was concerned with the search for enlightenment while Rahu in this life is bound by service to humanity, trying to fulfil the role imposed on it by the limitations of human birth.

Lessons of Virgo/Pisces axis: Ketu has to temporarily forget its spiritual aspirations and move towards service to the needs of the physical body in the sign of Virgo. The lesson of Rahu in Virgo is to treat every minor task, however mundane, as an expression of divinity. The work of Rahu and Ketu in this axis is to prepare the soul for its future spiritual expression. For it to connect properly there has to be an emphasis on karma yoga and an acceptance of this incarnation as a divine expression.

Mercury is neutral towards Jupiter, which treats it as an enemy. Rahu in Virgo is comfortable with the past life issues represented by Ketu in Pisces, but Ketu does not allow Rahu to forget its spiritual roots. This is the conflict of the axis. The spiritual needs continually intrude on the day to day life of an individual. Jupiter as the guru will try to block the material growth of Mercury and Virgo, but Mercury's nature is very adaptable and it can easily change to be in harmony with the Jupiterean dictates.

Rahu in Libra/Ketu in Aries
Rahu in Libra learns about balance, relationships, judgement and the good things of life. It does not know much about balance as it only deals with intense and obsessive emotions. Rahu is demonic, but Libra's ruler Venus is the celestial advisor to the demons and consequently helps Rahu finds its equilibrium without losing its inherent qualities. Libra is about relationships and Rahu needs to learn about others and about giving rather than taking. This is a good position for Rahu to be in. It tempers the need to establish relationships with other spiritual desires and gives a strong sense of justice.

Ketu in Aries gives you a fiery personality both physically and mentally. You have the qualities of a spiritual warrior and are happy to search for your spiritual roots in different parts of the world. There is always a new way of understanding your spirituality. But problems are created in worldly issues as you learn to let go of your individuality, reject your own needs and try to live for others.

Past life issues: Ketu is a spiritual warrior and Mars a physical one. The past life was a campaign fought for freedom and expression of the spiritual self, where failure was a foreign word. The individual prowess was attuned to achieving impossible goals. It was essentially a masculine/dynamic energy.

Lessons of Aries/Libra axis: Rahu in Libra is about balance and Ketu in Aries is about the self. Libra is a social sign and Aries seeks thrills and adventure so Ketu will keep pioneering in the realm of spirit. This axis usually pulls between individual search and partnership issues. Both are important and both will vie for attention. The axis will connect if the soul is allowed its freedom while working in a material world. The soul learns here to take others into consideration.

Mars and Venus are neutral to each other suggesting that this axis can work well through little effort. They can work out issues together and not try to spoil the other's party. If these two planets are negatively placed however, they will become aggressive towards each other and create obstacles in the other's path. Venus usually strives for harmony and Mars for war, but Venus can become overly critical and Mars aggressively militant. You will have to work to sort out the axis by calming Mars and making Venus less judgmental.

Rahu in Scorpio/Ketu in Taurus

Rahu Ketu are debilitated in this axis indicating that they go against their soul purpose in these signs. It need not necessarily be negative however and one has to understand the deeper meanings of this placement. Rahu is essentially a materialistic planet that learns spiritual lessons through worldly experience. In Scorpio it finds itself in a mystical spiritual domain where its obsessive action needs to experience the impulse of Scorpio intensely. As Scorpio can reveal hidden facets, both negative and positive, Rahu's placement here can become fraught with danger. Not recognising any boundaries, Rahu can overstep the mark in this occult area and find that the exciting new experiences have become hazardous and complicated. Like experiencing a new spiritual teacher or taking a new drug, Rahu's inherent thirst can soon become an addiction. With Rahu in Scorpio, you have to be forever careful what you let yourself get into. More than any other position of Rahu, here one must control and discipline its energy.

Ketu in Taurus is in a materialistic sign whereas its natural instinct is otherworldly. Ketu becomes very uncomfortable experiencing what it feels it must reject. Taurus has the beautiful quality of being neutral or *sama* - a nurturing and creative impulse that will nurture Ketu's spirituality. As the advisor to the demons Venus will harmonise with Ketu, but it is the virulence of Rahu that disturbs this axis.

Past life Issues: Ketu in Taurus indicates a past life full of sensuous comforts and physical enjoyments, the soul lost in the material realm. But Ketu is unhappy with this information and brings to the current life a sense of guilt over enjoying its pleasures; it creates a search for immediate fulfilment. This stimulates an urgency in Rahu to experience spirituality intensely and seek instant karma here.

The lessons of Scorpio/Taurus axis: There are no easy answers to the conflicts created here. The natural instinct is to search restlessly for a fast track to moksha, perhaps through cults and spiritual gurus, with the danger of getting sucked into a spiritual vortex or void. At the same time as the search for inner peace and happiness, there can be strong sexual longings and a need to fulfil your creative potential as you seek relationships and material happiness from your past life. You can either live a polarised life or understand the soul's secret. The journey towards enlightenment is long and eventful and it is not possible to find it in one lifetime alone. Ketu in Taurus should strive to feel comfortable in its material role as it is part of the learning process, and Rahu in Scorpio should try to calm down and learn to harness and control its energy.

Mars and Venus together denote passion. Here the axis creates multiple desires. Venus will be the calming influence on the fiery Ketu and Mars an aggravating one on Rahu. The strength of Mars and Venus will help this axis along, but if they are negatively placed to each other it can create havoc. I feel that whatever the quality of Mars and Venus in your chart, you need to handle this energy with care. It can be very special if properly understood. (Read the chapter on remedial measures for making the best of this axis.)

Rahu in Sagittarius/Ketu in Gemini

Sagittarius represents the stage of evolution where man learns to control his darker emotions. Rahu placed here can sometimes over-emphasise the darker side of the personality as Rahu is never totally comfortable with the Jupiterean impulse. In ancient times Rahu in Sagittarius was not appreciated as it indicated a person who might step away from traditional philosophy and religion and embrace negative foreign views. But today international views and philosophies influence all of us and therefore Rahu in Sagittarius will not be so difficult. Nevertheless the shadowy world of Rahu gets confused in the brightness of Sagittarius. There can be an attachment to the lower desires as Sagittarius rules the base chakra and here the kundalini starts rising. If the power of Rahu is not properly disciplined, the kundalini can rise viciously, creating problems with sexuality. Inside there may be fear and emotional trauma while the outer persona remains that of a teacher and a philosopher.

Ketu in Gemini is not totally at ease either. Gemini is the sign of intellect while Ketu is headless and therefore does not rationalise. Although Ketu is comfortable with Mercury, it will never be totally happy to focus on an individual ego. Ketu feels from the heart, knowing instinctively what is right or wrong. The separation from the absolute that takes place in Gemini is the very opposite to Ketu's basic need, so it will fight this impulse and try to impose its intuitive nature on Gemini. If accepted this is beneficial and can make the person an intellectually intuitive and unusual thinker, but if rejected the person can be a very narrow thinker, limited in the mental sphere.

Past Life Issues: Ketu in Gemini shows a past life spent in exploring the mind and the ambiguity of nature. There was a deep dissatisfaction with the experience of life leading to a current lack of recognition of its mental strength.

Lessons of Sagittarius/Gemini axis: Rahu has a powerful role in Sagittarius as it shapes the spiritual destiny of man - it can be the demonic teacher or the great politician. Its aspiration is of the highest, but sometimes it takes you to the lower paths to teach you a lesson about yourself - and this can be a divine blessing if properly understood. Ketu in Gemini may be intellectually myopic or intuitively excellent but it will never take the traditional path. It needs to let go of the intellectual parameters, while Rahu needs to be aware of the important role it has to perform, or both polarities will be blocked by each other's shortcomings. As Ketu relaxes its boundaries and allows intuition to flow it will guide Rahu to its higher purpose.

Mercury is neutral towards Jupiter, which treats it as an enemy. As Ketu is ruled by Mercury here it will be able to connect with Jupiter-ruled Rahu, but Jupiter's initial distrust of Mercury will not let itself be influenced. Ketu will need to keep working on the influences of Rahu in Sagittarius. At times Ketu will instinctively know that Rahu is not taking the right path, but Rahu's Jupiterean rulership will want to think for itself and reject advice. When Rahu learns to trust its instincts, the connection is made between the polarities and you can embark on the journey of your life.

Rahu in Capricorn/Ketu in Cancer
Rahu in Capricorn is about responsibility, both physical and psychological. Saturn rules Capricorn and Rahu has the character of Saturn on a psychological level so this placement is very strong. Capricorn insists on facing up to its karmic responsibilities before it can move into a more spiritual mode and Rahu's fear of failure results in pushing itself harder. Capricorn disciplines the wayward Rahu and this can give you great success in your chosen field as you combine hard work with high ambition. But at times it can be a lonely existence if achieving goals becomes an obsession and like a workaholic you do not know how to stop. Rahu in Capricorn needs to put some relaxation and fun in its schedule.

Ketu in Cancer is about coming to terms with your emotional nature. This is an extremely sensitive position which can bring unhappiness if you allow yourself to be ruled by your emotions. When you start looking beyond your own needs and turn the emotion to compassion, you will find great strength in making this work for others. As Cancer represents the soul moving from spiritual to material, Ketu can hesitate in moving into the material realm. But Ketu in Cancer has a lot to teach as it brings its mystical power into the everyday world.

Past Life Issues: Ketu in Cancer shows a soul very much connected to past lives. There is instinctive knowledge that can be trusted and this instinct develops with age. Following social dictates, the energy of our youth does not allow us to fully trust our knowledge, but with time we start allowing the instinct to flow and use the past knowledge to connect with today. Rahu in Capricorn gives this a positive form and much of its work is concerned with turning the instinctive desires into reality.

Lessons of Capricorn/Cancer axis: This axis can be very positive if you learn to fulfil your inner needs in the outer world. You have to develop a sense of detachment and treat life as a journey, where externalising your desires should be an element of the divine path. Making your desires come true is part of this axis but at the same time it is essential to avoid feeling disappointed when those dreams are realised. The danger of feeling that there are still further mountains to climb and that your journey so far has been useless will create a cycle of actions and disappointments. For this axis to connect you need to look back and take pleasure from your present achievements. Avoid saying to yourself 'I will only be happy if I achieve so and so.' Learn to enjoy the pleasures of today, however trivial.

Saturn is inimical to the Moon, which treats it as neutral, having no enemies of its own. This suggests that Rahu will not react well to the instinctive knowledge of Cancerian Ketu, and will not feel that it has to fulfil the needs carried over from the past life. Ketu wants Rahu to acknowledge this, which can create a block in the transfer of past life needs to the present life. This difficult relationship can only be resolved when Rahu in Capricorn recognises and acknowledges its past life and allows room for its feelings and instincts.

Rahu in Aquarius/Ketu in Leo

Rahu is considered by some classical astrologers to be the co-ruler of Aquarius. Aquarius is an air sign and so is Rahu. Rahu also acts like Saturn, the ruler of Aquarius, so this is a sign where the Rahu power is allowed its maximum expression. The symbol of Aquarius is a pitcher holding water. The pitcher represents the outer boundary and limitation of the human condition which ultimately has to break to allow the soul to merge back into infinity. Therefore Aquarius represents both the soul's entanglement in materialism and the ability to break the pitcher and move towards higher realms. Rahu in Aquarius can be both materialistic and spiritual. On a material path it can be given so much success that it feels overwhelmed, but eventually the dissatisfaction makes it seek its spiritual roots. Usually Rahu in Aquarius has the material aspiration first and only after this achievement does it aspire towards the spiritual.

Ketu in Leo is ruled by the Sun, which is a complicated relationship because Ketu eclipses the Sun yet the Sun also helps Ketu to express itself. As Ketu is only visible on the day of a solar eclipse it will naturally try to hide or block Leo's power and individuality. In this position it takes Ketu a long time to come to terms with power. Ketu in Leo is very strong once it stops trying to give away its power and starts to bring out its hidden capabilities. This is about the fire, aspiration, and intellect that becomes hidden under veils of material pursuit.

Past Life Issues: Ketu in Leo would have been a powerful personality in a past life, but somehow it finds it difficult to express the power in this life. People with this placement in their chart spend time ignoring their power, rejecting their beauty, and allowing others to dominate. They often project their personality through work done for others. Ketu in Leo is about bringing past life strength into this life.

Lessons of Aquarius/Leo axis: Rahu in Aquarius can become totally entangled in materialistic pursuits, but this materialism was from another time, another life. Similarly Rahu in Aquarius gives financial success which if misused can lead to disillusionment and disappointment. When the axis is disconnected, the individual struggles to come to terms with their personal ambitions, but when Ketu in Leo starts to use its strong personality for others, it feels comfortable about its inherent power and knowledge. This axis is all about using your power to make the world a better place to live.

The relationship between the Sun and Saturn is a difficult one. The father-son relationship in the astrological myths suggests than either Saturn or the Sun will be powerful at any one time, but not both. As in a human father-son situation, when the father is strong, the son (who is young) is weak. As the son gains his own strength, the father gets older and weaker, so this axis can suffer from opposing pulls with one end dominating the other at different times of life. By its very nature it tends to bring conflict in early years, but as Sun-Saturn and Rahu Ketu are all karmically linked, they have to learn to live together.

Rahu in Pisces/Ketu in Virgo

Pisces is an extremely mystical sign and Rahu's placement here is not ideal. While Rahu's search for idealism is fine, it is the area in which the quest is conducted that creates the problems. Rahu starts its search in the material world, hoping that success, money and sensual pleasures will give the answers. In fact what it creates is more questions. This does not mean that Rahu cannot find material happiness - it just has to look in the right places. The outer world is an illusion set to beguile us but ultimately leaves us incomplete. The completion that Rahu in Pisces desires comes from the spiritual journey within. Once the inner search begins, an understanding of the soul's purpose is within reach, taking the seeker to heights that others have rarely experienced.

In a way this Rahu Ketu axis is upside down, because Rahu in Pisces will be searching through the spiritual realm without understanding the true essence of it, perhaps creating disturbances in the mind. Pisces is the sign of moksha, and Rahu's ultimate aim is finding enlightenment, so although the role of Pisces and Rahu appear different their inner motivation is the same. Rahu in Pisces can be a beautiful experience if you learn to let go of pre-conceived ideas and allow the Piscean instinct to take over.

Virgo is a materialistic sign and Ketu is a spiritual planet so this is naturally an uncomfortable position for Ketu too. Ketu tries to search for its spiritual answers in the material world which creates dissatisfaction, as the detachment sought is not always possible. Virgo is a practical sign of service and Ketu is idealistic and impractical and only finds fulfilment by letting go of a personal agenda - this can be a problem.

Past Life Issues: Ketu in Virgo indicates a past life restricted by material concerns, and the struggle against these restrictions still binds the soul in this life. Rahu reflects the same issues but firstly pursues a material goal until it realises that spiritualism and enlightenment can be part of the agenda. At this point Rahu can change your psyche and enable you to progress onto the next level of soul development.

Lessons of Pisces/Virgo axis: This axis allows you to realise that you are able to move the soul onto the next level of maturity. Rahu in Pisces is at last in a situation where there are no emotional boundaries to spiritual success. As you learn to let go of your pre-conceived ideas, you realise that the restrictions were man-made ones, most of them erected in a previous life and no longer of any use now. You are able to move into a place of peace and true enlightenment - of coming to terms with yourself and being at peace with whatever the set of circumstances life has thrown at you.

Mercury is neutral towards Jupiter but is treated as an enemy. Ketu in Virgo is more comfortable with past life issues, which is why you are often pulled back into a life of service and restriction rather than being free to move into a more blissful Piscean state. As the ruler of Pisces, Jupiter will take a long time to understand that the Virgo agenda of Ketu and Mercury is from a past life, a distrust which leads to a disconnection between Rahu and Ketu. Rahu searches for perfection in the material world which it will understand when it is able to connect to Mercury-ruled Ketu and a state of happiness. Through a massive churning of emotions, the Pisces/Virgo axis has the capacity to bring bliss.

Analysing the Rashi Axis

The important factors in analysing Rahu Ketu by their sign placements are as follows:

1.   The signs that rule the axis. (For example Rahu Ketu are in the signs of Taurus and Scorpio).
2.   The planets that rule the sign - also known as the dispositors. (In the above example Venus is the dispositor or ruler of Taurus and Mars is the dispositor or the ruler of Scorpio).
3.   The relationship of the planet with its sign placement. Planets are subject to a five-fold relationship with a sign: exaltation, debilitation, mooltrikona, friends, and enemies. (For example Mars in Leo is 'friends', while Venus in Cancer is 'enemies'. See explanation and table below for clarification).
4.   The relative position of the dispositors to each other. Planets placed in the 6th, 8th and 12th houses from each other stop the flow of mutual positive energy. (If Mars is in Leo and Venus is in Cancer then Venus resides in the 12th house from Mars. This creates a lack of understanding between the past life Mars issues and the immediate Venusian ones).
5.   The dispositors' relationship with each other. Mars and Venus are neutral to each other - indicating both positive and negative aspects to deal with in this axis.
6.   The dispositors' relationship to the ascendant - is it a benefic or malefic planet for the ascendant? (For example Rahu in the 9th house will be powerful as its dispositor has the capacity to do well for the Ascendant. In the same way it can create problems in negative houses).

Ancient classics differ in interpretation of sign and house positions of the nodes. Rahu is negatively placed in the 4th but is considered well placed in Cancer. Rahu is good in Aries but negative on the Ascendant, so it is important to look at Rahu Ketu from both an esoteric and a practical point of view. Depending on your chosen path, Rahu's placement in a sign could be either negative or positive. If you are new to vedic astrology I suggest you read my book *The Essentials of Vedic Astrology*. This will explain the principles of planetary relationships and give a more complete picture of the science.

Natural Planetary Relationships

Each planet has friendship, enmity, or a neutral relationship with other planets. The rulers of the signs which are 2nd, 4th, 5th 8th, 9th, and 12th from the mooltrikona (special degrees of power) sign of the planets are its friends. Rulers of the signs other than the above are enemies. If planets rule more than one sign and have both a friendly and an inimical relationship, they become neutral.

The Planet	Its friends	Neutral	Its enemies
Sun	Moon, Mars, Jupiter	Mercury	Venus, Saturn
Moon	Sun, Mercury	Mars, Jupiter, Venus, Saturn	None
Mars	Sun, Moon, Jupiter	Venus, Saturn	Mercury
Mercury	Sun, Venus	Mars, Jupiter, Saturn	Moon
Jupiter	Sun, Moon, Mars	Saturn	Mercury, Venus
Venus	Mercury, Saturn	Mars, Jupiter	Sun, Moon
Saturn	Venus, Mercury	Jupiter	Sun, Moon, Mars
Rahu and Ketu	Mercury, Venus, Saturn	Mars	Sun, Moon, Jupiter

Exaltation and Debilitation

In certain signs of the zodiac the planets are considered to be in their optimum position. This is known as being in 'exaltation'. Opposite this is the sign of debilitation, where the planet is at its weakest. *Mooltrikona* are special degrees within signs that empower planets.

Planet	Exaltation	Mooltrikona	Debilitation	Rules
Sun	10° Aries	04-20° Leo	10° Libra	Leo
Moon	03° Taurus	04-20° Taurus	03° Scorpio	Cancer
Mars	28° Capricorn	00-12° Aries	28° Cancer	Aries, Scorpio
Mercury	15° Virgo	16-20° Virgo	15° Pisces	Gemini Virgo
Jupiter	05° Cancer	1-10° Sag	05° Capricorn	Sagittarius Pisces
Venus	27° Pisces	0-15° Libra	27° Virgo	Taurus, Libra
Saturn	20° Libra	0-20° Aquarius	20° Aries	Capricorn Aquarius

Rahu and Ketu are given exaltation points in Taurus/Scorpio and debilitation in Scorpio/Taurus. Gemini and Virgo are also given as exalted locations for Rahu and Ketu - no degree is given.

Relative Placement of Planets

Planets that are placed in the 6th, 8th and 12th house from each other prevent the axis from working smoothly - there will be struggles. Planets in a 5th and 9th house placement from each other will make the relationship flow smoothly. Planets in the 4th, 7th and 10th from each other show learning through stress and opposition. Planets in the 3rd and 11th from each other can be problematic but can work beautifully with a bit of concentration. Oppositions will make this axis further polarised, while conjunctions to the axis ruler will intensify the situation and you may find it hard to let go of issues.

6

Past Lives and Soul Lessons

The nakshatras are the guardians of the soul through its various journeys in different lives - as stars in the sky they remain passive observers. The nakshatra zodiac is the most ancient way of looking at astrology. When the nodal axis activates the nakshatras our karmic inheritances are brought to light and issues buried deep within our psyche are reflected in the mind. The nakshatras give you the final answer in unlocking your nodal axis.

There are 27 nakshatras, which being an uneven number means they do not fall easily into opposing pairs. For instance, when Rahu is in Ashwini, Ketu can be in either Chitra or Swati, which gives 54 possible axis polarities. Neither do the nakshatras fit neatly into signs: Vishakha is from 26°40 Libra to 3°20 Scorpio so there will be some crossover. The signs indicate the basic issues that are being dealt with, while the nakshatras show the deeper pattern. Ketu's attachment to past life baggage needs the impetus of Rahu to move on – and it needs to recognise that Rahu is honouring its own part of the karmic bargain by concentrating on opposing needs. What was left undone in the past become the desires of today. Understanding the nodal influence through the nakshatras allows us to reconcile our emotional crises and find happiness.

Rahu in Ashwini (0°00 to 13°20 Aries) and
Ketu in Chitra (0°00 to 6°40 Libra) or
Swati (6°40 to 13°20 Libra)

The Aries/Libra axis will always involve relationship issues in some form or another. Aries desires independence, while Libra wants partnership and togetherness. Depending on where the nodal axis falls, these needs will be either nurtured or antagonised, and there are different lessons in each.

Ashwini is named after the Ashwins, the twin sons of the Sun God. The Sun represents the parent, the root, the absolute. The Ashwins are the harbingers of dawn, so they can be seen as the link between the darkness and the light. Dawn brings the special energy of a new tomorrow which still has a connection to what has gone before – but Rahu placed here causes us to feel only the present as the dominant force. Rahu in Ashwini can live totally in the present, happy to indulge itself in the matters of today, but will ultimately find satisfaction through acknowledging its past. In India we believe that past lives fashion our future, and this philosophy is strongly indicated in the first nakshatra. Ketu is the ruler of Ashwini and so it is Rahu's invisible half. The independence and restlessness typical of Rahu in Ashwini is the search for the secret personality, the hidden potential. The divine link of the Sun, Rahu and Ketu to the first nakshatra indicates that there is an important evolutionary process in operation here. However, it may create much confusion and pain until you learn to direct the search into the proper channels.

The conflict between Ashwini and Chitra
Chitra means a reflection or a beautiful picture and thus it reflects the potential of the soul. The symbol of Chitra is a pearl, and pearls are found in hard shells. Until the shell is broken, the true lustre can not emerge. Nature takes a very long time to create a pearl, and translated to human terms it means there may be many lifetimes before the pearl within a person can appear. Breaking the shell is a difficult process and usually means that an individual must make immense changes before their true personality can shine through.

Ketu in Chitra teaches us to control our passions and direct them towards a more divine goal. In a past life you learnt to express your spiritual core by breaking away from the traditions and restrictions imposed by society. Ketu gave you the courage to begin your search for self-realisation.

The Ashwini Chitra axis can be complicated. Rahu in Ashwini denies its spiritual link and Ketu in Chitra denies its material link, which can lead to emotional dissatisfaction. The resolution to this lies with Rahu - especially as Ketu rules Ashwini and Rahu is in Ashwini. The conflict of Ashwini Chitra is about understanding the other - trying to encompass what feels uncomfortable – and once the fear of losing our own identity is seen as unfounded, we are on the way to resolving karmic disharmony.

The conflict between Ashwini and Swati
Swati means sword and it symbolises a tool for self-advancement, cutting through the competition on its way to success. Swati is also the name of the wife of the Sun, so in Swati the Sun forgets its spiritual purpose and becomes involved in

the pleasures and pains of relationship. For a moment it is not bothered about moksha or enlightenment. As Rahu rules Swati, Ketu's placement here shows a past in which you struggled with the dilemma of relationships versus the trappings of success. Swati is a nakshatra connected to Artha or practical considerations and Ketu feels very uncomfortable in this environment. It tries to turn its life towards spiritualism, but material issues will always dominate.

Rahu Ketu in the Ashwini Swati axis is confusing because Ashwini is the dawn, the link from the past to the present, and Rahu Ketu are the invisible links from past to present. Rahu placed in Ashwini is ruled by Ketu and Ketu placed in Swati is ruled by Rahu - so they are placed in their opposing nakshatras, creating karmic confusion. Rahu in Ashwini is busy pursuing a false dawn while Ketu in Swati is rejecting relationships to try to justify the need for moksha. Both of them are rejecting their partners - their reasons may appear different - but the end result is the same. The answer lies in understanding each other's issues. Ketu in Swati should understand that working through relationships is just as valid a path to moksha as a spiritual one, and Rahu in Ashwini must learn to recognise their soul partners.

To understand Rahu in Ashwini with the two nakshatra positions of Ketu, the relative position of Mars and Venus in the natal chart should be viewed. This will indicate how you can re-establish a connection of the nodes and fulfil the hidden demands of your psyche.

Rahu in Bharani (13°20 to 26°40 Aries) and
Ketu in Swati (13°20 to 20°00 Libra) or
Vishakha (20°00 to 26°40 Libra)

Rahu in Bharani will have Ketu placed in either Swati or Vishakha. Although Bharani is placed in Aries, the sign of Mars, it is ruled by Venus. *Bharani* means cherishing, supporting and nourishing, and it expresses feminine energy in its purist form. Bharani is the sensualist of the zodiac, a quality greatly enhanced by the presence of Rahu. The strong Venusian influence makes this nakshatra one of intense attraction and desire for sexual expression, but partnerships can become so extremely important that we fear a life without sensual expression. The ruling deity of Bharani is Yama, the god of death. But the 'death' is not purely physical. Yama allows us to detach ourselves from previous lives so that we can look ahead and sow the seed for the future. In Yoga, *yama* (restraint) and *niyama* (practice or observation) are disciplines used to channel the energies of the organs of action and perception in the right direction. Rahu in Bharani is tempted to forget about its past and revel in the present, and must learn some discipline if it is to avoid unrestrained excess. Rahu in Bharani, practising yama and niyama, has the capacity to use this power whichever way it wants.

The conflict between Bharani and Swati

Both Bharani and Swati are connected to relationships, which further highlights the Aries/Libra axis. Bharani is essentially sensuous and Swati is about marriage and commitment, but Rahu in Bharani desires relationships while Ketu in Swati rejects them. Rahu has to experience and express the sexual urges fully while Ketu really doesn't want to get involved. The result can be a relentless pursuit of sex followed by a total rejection of intimacy and commitment.

This is a potentially confusing combination as Rahu is placed in a nakshatra ruled by Venus and in a sign that rules Ketu, and Ketu is placed in a nakshatra ruled by Rahu and a sign ruled by Venus. It can feel like any action you take leads towards another question. This nodal axis can create deep anxieties about relationships and your inability to fulfil the demands of the others. Your natural reaction to pain is to reject your partner but this experience is a very important part of the soul's growth and its fears about relating are no longer valid. It is vital to study the positions of Mars and Venus in your chart, and also how Rahu is placed in relationship to Venus and Ketu is placed in relationship to Mars. Learn to trust your relationships. (Here I am suggesting all relationships, not just sexual or intimate ones). Swati may also use its sword-like qualities to cut off from materialism too, but you should remember that much of the conflict with both relationship and materialist issues has already been acted out in past lives.

The conflict between Bharani and Vishakha

Visha means to enter and *Kha* means Heaven, so Visha-kha together means to aspire to enter the gates of heaven. Ketu also aspires to its place in heaven, and as Jupiter is the planetary ruler it gives wisdom to move towards a spiritual life. Ketu in Vishakha suggests that in a past life the soul understood the knowledge of moksha, but the life was essentially human and full of material and sexual issues. Many unfulfilled desires were therefore brought into this life resulting in a sense of dissatisfaction. The soul has made a commitment to begin a deeper search but has yet to experience what it is seeking.

Both Bharani and Vishakha have strong sexual issues. Bharani is overtly sensuous but Vishakha's energy is not so immediately obvious. Vishakha's animal sign is the Tiger, a powerful animal and a strong sexual symbol. This can create sensual obsessions, but as the spiritual aspect of Vishakha is connected to being on a threshold you also stand at the gateway of new possibilities.

The placement of Jupiter and Venus in your chart will show which way this conflict will be resolved. Both these gurus are there to guide you. Venus and Jupiter are spiritual teachers who can work both positively or negatively in your life - the choice is yours. The strength of Jupiter or Venus indicates whether

Rahu or Ketu will dominate, but the conflict of this axis must be resolved in the material life. The obvious consumption and consumerism that both these nakshatras create can be broken by learning to express your spirituality in the everyday world. This will avoid you creating karmic debt in future lives.

Rahu in Krittika (26°40 Aries to 10°00 Taurus) and Ketu in Vishakha (26°40 Libra to 3°20 Scorpio) or Anuradha (3°20 to 10°00 Scorpio)

Rahu in Krittika will have Ketu placed in either Vishakha or Anuradha. Krittika is ruled by the Sun and Vishakha is ruled by Jupiter. Krittika is the puritan of the zodiac while Vishakha is both sensuous and spiritual. Rahu is an enemy of the Sun and has the capacity to eclipse it when placed in Krittika. This can mean a struggle with darker forces before you find the true light, but remember it is only during an eclipse that you get a glimpse of Rahu. Signs and nakshatras ruled by the Sun have the capacity to bring out that rare and divine quality of Rahu that is otherwise hidden in the world of matter. Rahu in Krittika is in its exalted sign of Taurus and can use its power for the best of purposes. It can reveal its secret nature or be a difficult inheritance. It will incubate the seed of Rahu and bring forth its potential whichever way you allow it to develop, placing the responsibility of how you are going to lead your life firmly on yourself. Rahu in Krittika is passive and can be either constructive or destructive.

The conflict between Krittika (Aries) and Vishakha (Libra)

Ketu brings all its past life experiences to the fore in Vishakha and lets you stand at the threshold of the new. Now you have the ability to make what you want from life. Vishakha's symbol is the potter's wheel – an energy that contrasts immense activity on the outside to a centre that remains static. Ketu in Vishakha suggests a past life that was full of noise, drama and action, yet the inner soul was silent and centred, bringing aspirations to do the right thing into this life. Ketu may try to reject the material needs of Vishkha in order to create its spiritualising influence.

As the rulers of these nakshatras are friends (Jupiter and the Sun), the conflict of Krittika and Vishakha can be minimised. Also both nakshatras have the same deity in Agni - the god of fire. Agni represents the seven flames which allow the seven levels of consciousness to operate. It is the kundalini, the latent fire that rests in the spine, and Agni is strongly connected to the self-discipline of yoga. It is the fire of the mind, the flames of aspiration and the blaze of intellect that burn away the negative sheaths so that we emerge pure. This Rahu Ketu axis can take you through an experience of fire to bring out your best qualities. If it is left uncontrolled you can burn yourself out, but if you control the energy you can awaken your kundalini fire and bring about your own transformation. The rulership of Krittika in Aries gives dominance to Rahu in this axis as both Mars and Sun are friends to each other. But Krittika is a passive nakshatra and it can allow Rahu to develop uncontrolled if you do not understand its spiritual capacity.

The conflict between Krittika (Taurus) and Vishakha (Scorpio)

Here the axis is still Rahu in Krittika ruled by the Sun and Ketu in Vishakha ruled by Jupiter, but the zodiac signs have changed to Taurus/Scorpio and with it the whole impact of Rahu Ketu. The central issue has moved from relationships to the attractions of the material world versus the desire for spiritual growth. Some combinations will prove easier to work with than others.

Krittika, now in Taurus, comes under the guidance of Venus. The Sun and Venus are enemies so Rahu in Krittika in Taurus will not be able to express itself with the same ease as it did in Aries. However Ketu in Vishakha is now in the sign of Scorpio, where it is exalted. Ketu is said to act like Mars, so although it never feels completely at home with the conservative attitude of Jupiter, its energy in this part of the axis has more harmony and less conflict. The individual feels more comfortable with their past life issues than with those of the present, and struggles with the opposing influences of Sun and Venus. Ketu in Vishakha shows a past life connection where the kundalini was being slowly awakened to begin the search for fulfilment, and the mysterious Scorpio focuses on the deep spiritual self. But Rahu in Krittika Taurus is not in its easiest placement despite its exaltation in this sign.

The conflict between Krittika and Anuradha

Anuradha means a tiny spark - it takes only a small flash of intuition or a tiny spark of consciousness to bring awareness of our connection to the divine. Anuradha unveils this hidden purity and Ketu in Anuradha indicates that it was in a past life that we opened our mind to the kundalini. Saturn's rulership of Anuradha shows that many karmic responsibilities were paid for in the past life, and that now it is time to learn from the past life lessons, transfer the spark to Rahu in Krittika and bring out our special qualities.

Krittika is ruled by the Sun and Anuradha is ruled by Saturn, the rejected son of the Sun god, so the relationship between father and son may be important in this life. Saturn also represents democracy in contrast to the Sun's absolute power. This nakshatra axis highlights the mental struggles between your past and present. You may feel that the path chosen in the previous life, where you learnt to give up your personal authority, was better than the present. Ketu in Anuradha may want to block the growth of Rahu in Krittika, fearing corruption by absolute power, but if the individual remains disconnected to the present, the valuable karmic lessons from the past can not be utilised. Ketu has to teach the lessons of democracy and discipline to Rahu.

Rahu in Rohini (10°00 to 23°20 Taurus) and Ketu in Anuradha (10°00 to 16°40 Scorpio) or Jyeshta (16°40 to 23°20 Scorpio)

Rahu in Rohini will have Ketu placed in either Anuradha or Jyeshta. In Sanskrit the word Rohini means red, a colour that relates to passion and sensuality. The inner core of Rohini is full of emotion, romanticism and love. They may not admit it to everyone, but those with this placement have lots of love to give and Rahu in Rohini can become a relentless search to experience love in many dimensions. They seek a partner through whom they can find the ultimate answers to life, which is of course a tall order. To avoid the restless search, Rahu in Rohini should try to experience every facet of love from a single relationship in order to learn the lessons of true love and happiness that their soul craves. Rohini is ruled by the Moon, but has the power to eclipse it. In some ways Rahu in Rohini can cause you to feel blocked on a soul level fearing change and transformation, but the value of the Moon Rahu relationship can be understood in terms of a lunar eclipse: Rahu transforms the Moon by eclipsing it, bringing the soul into a new domain where different ideas flourish and the order of life changes. On a spiritual level, Rohini transports the soul to the material realm in comfort, protecting it while it gets ready to face its earthly responsibilities.

The conflict between Rohini and Anuradha
Anuradha unveils the latent potential that has become hidden by a life centred on materialism. This potential is the ability to give divine love unconditionally. Ketu's placement here indicates that this process was dominant in past lives, where materialism was rejected to find the spiritual ideal. Both Rohini and Anuradha seek self-realisation through love, but the axis pulls in two different ways. Rohini seeks sexual love whereas Anuradha seeks the link to divine love. Anuradha is ruled by Saturn and is placed in Scorpio - where Ketu is exalted. But the Mars Saturn rulership shows the great struggle that Ketu's placement puts on the soul - trying to connect itself to the overtly material path of Rahu in Rohini while still tied to its need for moksha. Realising that the experience of true love in a purely physical form is as divine an act as its spiritual counterpart will solve the dilemma. The important fact is that Rahu in Rohini should not waste its energy in uncommitted sexual liaisons as this will cause frustration at a deep level.

The conflict between Rohini and Jyeshta

This axis suggests a universal pattern where the soul struggles intensely in one life to overcome its demons, then goes through a life where there is relative calm, before repeating the initial process in another life but this time with greater intensity. Jyeshta is an extremely powerful nakshatra because the soul breaks away from its materialistic course here and moves towards the final part of the journey. Jyeshta gives a person a strong sense of destiny where he has to struggle with his lower and higher desires. The ruler of Jyeshta is Mercury, the planet that provides the celestial link between materialism and spiritualism. Ketu in Jyeshta suggests that this soul struggle was very intense in a past life and that now it will express itself in the material realm – almost an experiment to see if the struggles of the past will stand the test of earthly life. Ketu in Jyeshta does not easily let go of the past, with the result that Rahu in Rohini continues to feel blocked. Rohini's ruling planet, the Moon, is emotional and Jyestha's ruler Mercury is analytical. This axis is considered to be the exaltation position of Rahu and Ketu, yet the emotional and spiritual conflict is intense in order to bring about the enlightenment that the nodes suggest. Trying to link the past spiritual advances to the material path that Rahu in Rohini has to tread makes this axis easier to deal with – don't forget your past, but do try to enjoy the material goods that are on offer now.

Rahu in Mrigasira (23°20 Taurus to 6°40 Gemini) and
Ketu in Jyeshta (23°20 to 30°00 Scorpio) or
Mula (0°00 to 6°40 Sagittarius)

Rahu in Mrigasira will have Ketu placed in either Jyeshta or Mula. *Mriga* means a deer and *Sira* means head, and the head of the deer is also a symbol of the Moon. Mrigasira is considered the nakshatra where the intellect is born and where the intellectual search begins. Rahu in Mrigasira will begin this search in the outside world, and if answers are not forthcoming it will quickly change track. This nakshatra is also ruled by Mars, the planet of action and adventure, so there will be adventure both intellectually and physically. The Rahu Mars relationship is always considered a difficult one because neither recognise boundaries and they are both extremely courageous, even foolhardy. The important aspect of Rahu's intellectual search is to prove that the answers we seek externally are not enough – and at that point the inner journey can begin.

The conflict between Mrigasira and Jyeshta

Jyeshta is connected to the kundalini, which when energised and correctly mastered gives immense powers to an individual. He can rule the world, communicate with the spirits, have the knowledge of past and future lives. In order to unfold the kundalini in the right way, you must go beyond the attachments of the physical world. Ketu in Jyeshta shows a past life where you tried to externalise this potential and use it in practical ways. Rahu in Mrigasira tries to intellectualize this process but by doing so is in a danger of becoming entangled once more with materialism.

Mercury and Mars are the rulers of these nakshatras, and they are not friends: this is a conflict between intellectual and spiritual power. Rahu in Mrigasira is trying to contain the awakened soul within intellectual barriers, but this does not allow its full expression. Although Rahu Ketu are considered to be exalted here, the soul really does struggle to connect and resolve its physical restrictions. If Ketu is in the last part of Jyeshta (26°40 to 30°00 Scorpio), it will be in *gandanta* (special karmic degrees), indicating an emotional knot that the soul was trying to unravel in a previous life. This knot forms part of your psychological makeup now and may create deep-rooted blocks to your development. The soul forces you to recognise your power and use it towards inner development rather than an outer search.

The conflict between Mrigasira and Mula

This is a power point of the nakshatra system. Mula is not only the root from which all spirituality flowers, but can also be the root that contains our negativity. Mula is the start of the final part of the soul's mission to find answers to lead to the breaking away from the cycles of life and death. Ketu in its own nakshatra suggests that the past life was spent aspiring towards spirituality which led to a change in the psychology of the individual. It now fulfils its role as the moksha planet by arousing the soul towards its ultimate destination. This is a very important incarnation for the individual with heavy soul responsibility.

Ketu rules Mula and Mars rules Mrigasira, and Ketu and Mars are similar. Mars is the physical warrior and Ketu the spiritual one, so here Mars can bring the needs of Ketu into the physical realm. Its ability to do so depends on its quality in your chart. Ketu brings the potential from previous lives to this one and places a great responsibility on Rahu to assimilate this information and use it correctly.

Rahu in Ardra (6°40 to 20°00 Gemini) and
Ketu in Mula (6°40 to 13°20 Sagittarius) or
Purva Ashadha (13°20 to 20°00 Sagittarius)

As the zodiac axis changes to Gemini/Sagittarius the quick thinking and constantly moving energy of Mercury can be confusing and unsatisfactory: the tremendous knowledge accrued in previous lives needs to find its way out so it can become of practical help in the physical world.

Rahu in Ardra will have Ketu placed in either Mula or Purva Ashadha. *Ardra* means green, moist and like a tear-drop. The moistness of the eyes can blur the picture yet we feel renewed and refreshed after tears have been shed. Rahu rules Ardra and represents the intellectual prowess represented by the sign of Gemini. The ruler is Mercury and the lust for immortality is Rahu, which left to its own devices can become too power-hungry and create a mist of confusion in the mind. At the cosmic stage of Ardra it is the dissatisfaction with our present surroundings that starts the search for answers, but it is possible to become confused and enlightened at the same time. However this can be an excellent position when you learn to use the positive traits of Rahu.

Rahu placed in Ardra has a double Rahu impact, and there is almost no getting from the conflict it represents. The symbol of Ardra is the head, thus linking the nakshatra to intellectual excellence - in fact most of Rahu 's challenges come from the mind, for it is your thinking that can guide you to the right or wrong paths. Rahu in Ardra sometimes tries too hard to succeed and ends up dominating others intellectually, or else it reaches for the impossible only to discover the futility of achievement. A search for intellectual perfection can make us dissatisfied with our current level of life.

The conflict between Ardra and Mula

Ketu in Mula is in its own nakshatra and creates a mirror effect, as if you are standing in front of a mirror with another mirror behind you. These multiple reflections are your past lives staring back at you and making a deep psychological impact. You must now try to bring their essence into your current lifetime. Ketu is rooted in earth and it grows towards the sky aspiring to enlightenment. It was unable to fulfil this aspiration in a previous life and still feels extremely unfulfilled now.

This is one the most intense zodiac positions for Rahu Ketu. Rahu in Ardra is ruled by Rahu itself and Ketu in Mula is ruled by Ketu. It shows a life that is bringing forward its karmic issues from a previous lifetime. All issues that were being worked on are still prevalent now. Although both Rahu and Ketu are well placed in Gemini-Sagittarius, it is in these particular degrees that the axis becomes all powerful. Vedic astrology does not favour Rahu or Ketu in their own nakshatras as they can create major psychological barriers to future growth. When you repeat patterns of a previous life you may well feel connected to destiny, but when the same events keep happening many times it can seem like you have no control. The remedial measures at the back of this book will help to guide you through this.

The strengths of the sign dispositors, Mercury and Jupiter, become very important for a true understanding of the Ardra Mula axis. The soul has to accept its role in the material life, not fight it. The physical restrictions that life places on us are part of the soul's mission. The flowering of the future allows the physical body to connect with the soul body.

The conflict between Ardra and Purva Ashadha
Purva means first and Ashadha means *unsubdued*, so this nakshatra indicates that which cannot be suppressed. The true nature of a person comes out regardless of the opposition they have to face. Ketu in Purva Ashada indicates uncovering our most valuable qualities from previous lives and externalising our inner strengths to find our true light. The previous lifetime was not without its difficulties, but Venus (the ruler of Purva Ashadha) smoothed the path and created situations where wisdom flourished. Rahu in Ardra wants to control life intellectually, yet these aspirations can block the path to personal happiness. In the same way Rahu in Ardra often feels dissatisfied as its achievements do not bring the happiness expected. Understanding that this is your greatest limitation will help. Ketu in Purva Ashadha feels frustrated that material issues have blocked its spiritual journey, yet a true understanding of the axis is this: It is the past life experience that has given Rahu in Ardra its sharp mind and now it has the ability to use the wisdom of experience for the good of others through higher thinking. As Rahu is in harmony with Purva Ashadha's ruler, Venus, it will connect with Ketu. The answers to your dissatisfaction lie now in the material world; as long as you search for light in the outer world, you will feel eclipsed or fearful within. But if you allow the instinctive knowledge that shone in previous lives to guide you, you can find peace and happiness.

Rahu in Punarvasu (20°00 Gemini to 3°20 Cancer) and Ketu in Purva Ashadha (20°00 to 26°40 Sagittarius) or Uttara Ashadha (26°40 Sagittarius to 3°20 Capricorn)

Rahu in Punarvasu will have Ketu placed in either Purva Ashadha or Uttara Ashadha. Punarvasu deals with the transfer of knowledge from the spiritual to the earthly plane, and Jupiter as the true teacher is responsible for guiding this process. Punarvasu deals with the wandering mind in search of its true identity. Those with Rahu in Punarvasu are forever searching at different levels of life. Once they find the answer to one level of manifestation - for example a material one – they will start a new search on the spiritual level, and so on. It is best to appreciate this restlessness for what it is or it could lead to a disappointment at not finding a final answer.

Punarvasu's ruling deity is Aditi, the universal mother who is infinite and cares for all. Rahu in Punarvasu creates a psychological need to mother and love others, but the expression remains in the mind and is rarely followed through. However the yearning for motherhood is strong. In a male chart, it can mean caring - like the idea of a 'modern' man. Rahu's placement here can exacerbate a fear of being emotionally detached or of lacking commitment and love from your mother. Punarvasu spans two signs – Gemini and Cancer. In Gemini the intellectual issues will rule while in Cancer the emotional instinct will be stronger. (Mercury's relationship with Jupiter is not always easy but Jupiter works well with the Moon).

The conflict between Punarvasu and Purva Ashadha
Purva Ashadha means that which cannot be suppressed. Ketu in Purva Ashadha shows that in a previous life the spiritual nature was unfolding whether you were trying to achieve this or not. Purva Ashadha developed knowledge and wisdom through soul experiences that cannot be taken away. As Jupiter (the ruler of Punarvasu) is inimical to Venus (the ruler of Purva Ashadha), there will not be much past life support for Rahu's search for happiness in the present life. The soul inheritance of wisdom and knowledge can be blocked. Punarvasu is searching for a new home in which the soul might find happiness but fails to understand that the soul is quite happy within itself, and it is the ever changing circumstances of life that are creating the illusion of unhappiness. Ketu in Purva Ashadha has gained immense perception and now forms Rahu's invisible half. People with Rahu in Punarvasu need to take time off from their astral or physical travels and look beyond their intellectual limitations. The moment they connect to their past life experiences they will be more at peace with their karma.

The conflict between Punarvasu (Gemini) and Uttara Ashadha (Sag)
Uttara Ashadha links to the previous nakshatra, Purva Ashadha. Together they represent the common principle of unfolding new talents. In Purva Ashadha there was the dawning of new psychological changes, and their assimilation into the psyche takes place in Uttara Ashadha, whose ruler the Sun signifies Atma or the soul. Ketu placed here shows a past life where the soul was almost ready to mature, so now is the time to leave the shadows behind; by expanding your mind you can embrace the subsconscious and allow the light to shine through.

The maturity of the soul as reflected by Ketu in Uttara Ashadha connects to the needs of Rahu in Punarvasu more easily here than in the previous axis. Jupiter and the Sun, the two rulers of this nakshatra axis, are friends; they help to integrate Ketu's knowledge with Rahu's experiences so the nodes are more in tune. At first Rahu uses the past life knowledge in its journey through the material realms, but when that knowledge does not fulfil, the psyche directs its search inwards. A cautionary warning is relevant here in that any inner journey should only be undertaken after physical preparation through yoga, meditation or a similar discipline, otherwise it can open up the mind to areas where it may be unable to cope.

The conflict between Punarvasu (Cancer) and Uttara Ashadha (Cap)

Rahu Ketu remain in the Punarvasu-Uttara Ashadha axis but the signs now change to Cancer and Capricorn. The influence of this axis will be very different to the previous one, for while the nakshatra rulers (Jupiter and Sun) are friends the sign rulers show different energies. The intimate nurturing of Cancer conflicts with the Capricorn desire to make a mark on the world and leave something of tangible value behind. Rahu in Punarvasu is now influenced by Jupiter and the Moon - two friends who are both sattvik planets and can influence Rahu positively. Ketu however is less happy in Uttara Ashadha due to the contradictory influence of the Sun and Saturn. The Sun is monarchy and Saturn democracy, and this conflict was sure to have influenced Ketu in a past life. It needs the support of right action now to bring about further transformation.

Rahu in Pushya (3°20 to 10°00 Cancer) and
Ketu in Uttara Ashadha (3°20 to 10°00 Capricorn) or
Shravana (10°00 to 16°40 Capricorn)

Rahu in Pushya will have Ketu placed in either Uttara Ashadha or Shravana. *Pushya* means to nourish or thrive and it works to nourish others and create conditions so that the world can thrive. Pushya is ruled by Saturn and situated in Cancer, which is ruled by the Moon. The connection of Saturn with the Moon impacts profoundly on the mind, and this is psychologically increased by Rahu's placement here. Rahu acts like Saturn and takes on its teachings about responsibility and discipline in order to search for the true light. Rahu in Pushya also recognises that this life is part of a whole, but not the whole in itself. Therefore there is a limited destiny to be experienced by the incarnating soul, connected to the growth and restrictions that Saturn represents. Rahu hates restrictions but faces them in Pushya. This can be a very frustrating experience if you find you are subconsciously resisting the challenge to grow.

The conflict between Pushya and Uttara Ashadha

Ketu in Uttara Ashadha is ruled by the Sun and placed in Capricorn. Again this is a relationship between Saturn and a Luminary. In a past life the Saturnian influence on the soul instigated the move towards moksha. The change was so profound and the inner need to leave the cycle of unhappiness behind so compelling, that Uttara Ashadha sometimes loses its knack of relating to the world.

The Sun and Moon are extremely inimical to the nodes and Saturn will focus all the attention on facing up to the karmic issues. Ketu in Uttara Ashadha highlights a past life where the soul accepted moksha as its final choice but Rahu in Pushya finds it difficult to connect to its past life. The relationship between the two nakshatra rulers is a difficult one. Saturn makes us aware of karma that has to be faced on earth but the Sun does not want to be tied to any restrictions. This can affect your mind as a feeling of intense loneliness even when surrounded by friends and loved ones. The important factor to remember here is that the loneliness is a past life karma, and that in this life you are having to deal with some responsibilities that were left over from before. Facing this karma leads to personal development and strength within.

The conflict between Pushya and Shravana

Shravana means listening and it is called the nakshatra of total silence. This silence allows us to see through the illusions of life. Ketu in this nakshatra indicates that the need for quietness and reflection was part of our previous life, and the silence of this total meditation brought a control to the wandering mind. The soul now searches for peace and silence in this life. This axis is connected strongly to the mind. Rahu is placed in Pushya (ruled by Saturn) in the sign of the Moon (Cancer). Ketu is in Shravana (ruled by the Moon) in the sign of Saturn (Capricorn). The nodal axis is forever connected to Moon-Saturn challenges. The Moon is the waxing, waning, ever-changing mind, while Saturn is the rigid teacher of truths. Saturn and the Moon are also related by their transits, as the Moon takes 29 ½ days to complete its orbit and Saturn takes 29 ½ years. The Moon is emotional and changeable - Saturn is disciplined, rigid and inflexible. It is Saturn that will teach us to control our emotions and be detached from the ups and downs of life; this forces us to take more responsibility for ourselves as we move from the silence of past lives to the cacophony of the present.

Rahu in Ashlesha (16°40 to 30°00 Cancer) and
Ketu in Shravana (16°40 to 23°20 Capricorn) or
Ketu in Dhanishta (23°20 to 30°00 Capricorn)

Rahu in Ashlesha will have Ketu placed in either Shravana or Dhanishta. Ashlesha means to 'embrace' and indicates the soul embracing life so that is can act out its karma. As soon as we embrace life we become subject to earthly rules and regulations, which of course includes the process of life and death, happiness and unhappiness. Destiny, born from our own actions in previous lives, influences the life today. Rahu in Ashlesha emphasizes this factor. While Rahu enjoys experiencing life, it soon becomes frustrated by the embrace of destiny and seeks for something more to fulfill its desires. This creates an imbalance psychologically, and as the ruler of Ashlesha is Mercury, the emphasis will be on the intellect.

Ashlesha is linked to the snake. Its presiding deity is the Nagas, the Sanskrit name for the snake, and its symbol is the serpent. Snakes shed their skin periodically and as Rahu as Vasuki is also a Naga, its placement in Ashlesha indicates a major psychological transformation during the course of this life. Rahu placed in the end degrees of Ashlesha is in a gandanta point, the karmic knot that is difficult to unravel. It is important if you have such a placement to concentrate on the inner development of your soul and not to force your spirituality until you are truly ready for it.

The conflict between Ashlesha and Shravana
Ketu in Shravana deals with intuition, silence and meditation, and is ruled by the Moon - the significator of the mind. The mind connects every level of consciousness, not just the intellectuality of Mercury. The ruling deity of Shravana is Vishnu, who is the light beyond our perception. Vishnu is considered one of the most important gods of the Vedas and forms the holy trinity with Shiva and Brahma. Vishnu means 'he who crosses heights'. He encourages his followers to cross the heights beyond capabilities, and Ketu's placement here suggests a past where Vishnu was the guiding force. You were developing the intuition and were in touch with this god.

The conflict of this axis is connected to the mind. Rahu in Ashlesha can be both intuitive and intelligent if it allows itself to connect with Ketu in Shravana. The knowledge that Rahu in Ashlesha desperately seeks is within its shadowy partner Ketu in Shravana. As Mercury, the ruler of Ashlesha, is inimical to the Moon, it does not trust the past life information. It wants to analyse everything and ignores the greater knowledge available in listening to the intuition. Many of the frustrations that Rahu brings would disappear if we learned to trust our intuition.

The conflict between Ashlesha and Dhanishta
Dhani means wealthy and *Ishta* means complete, so together Dhanishta means complete wealth - both in spirit and mind. Ketu in Dhanishta shows a past life where the soul worked hard to acquire this wealth through selfless work, letting go of the personal ego and working with compassion and high ideals. Ketu in Dhanishta also represents the inner cleansing of the soul in readiness to receive

divine music. It is this past life placement that connects to Rahu in Ashlesha and makes it want to leave the comfort of materialism for spiritual reality. Mercury and Mars, the respective rulers of these two nakshatras, are inimical to each other and past life knowledge is not easily understood. The soul needs to transform the active spiritual participation of the past life to a dynamic mental one. Rahu in Ashlesha must remember that any restrictions it faces in this powerful nakshatra are mental blocks erected by itself and that by truly embracing and transforming with Ashlesha energy it can find the fulfilment it seeks.

Rahu in Magha (0°00 to 13°20 Leo) and
Ketu in Dhanishta (0°00 to 6°40 Aquarius) or
Shatabhishak (6°40 to 13°20 Aquarius)

Rahu in Magha will have Ketu placed in either Dhanishta or Shatabhishak. *Magha* means mighty or great, and people born in this nakshatra aspire towards eminence and prominence in their chosen field. Magha is the beginning of the second cycle in the soul's journey, (the signs Leo to Scorpio indicate the soul's full involvement in the pleasures and pains of earthly life). Ketu, the significator of spiritual realisation ruling the commencing point of the materialistic journey, shows the importance of the experience of Tamas - the realities of life including illusion, darkness and attachment - in fulfilling the divine mission of the soul. Rahu is placed in its partner (Ketu's) sign, and can get confused about which path it needs to take. Rahu in Magha searches for success beyond expectation, and may use underhand means to make it happen. You have to be careful to be ethical, as you can easily block your own good qualities by feeling that becoming a prominent personality is all there is.

Rahu in Magha knows intuitively that material happiness is only an experience to develop the qualities of the soul. In itself Magha will be happy to express its divine mission in a practical way - it is only the placement of Rahu there that confuses the issue. Rahu can feel dissatisfied with this role for there is no definition of success. As the kind of success that Rahu in Magha desires is available to very few it feels unfulfilled - regardless of the fact that the world may consider the individual to be successful.

The conflict between Magha and Dhanishta

Ketu is in the part of Dhanishta that is placed in Aquarius, ruled by Saturn, and Mars rules Dhanishta. Mars and Saturn are opposing energies, one indicating bravery and action and the other restrictions. Saturn brings forth karma which must be faced at the appropriate time so that the past can be cleansed, but Mars wants to break through all spiritual barriers now. Ketu intensifies this need for enlightenment.

Rahu is in Magha ruled by Ketu, in the sign of Leo ruled by the Sun. The needs of the soul are paramount. Rahu has to use past life knowledge in the materialistic present, but this is often misunderstood by others who see your desire for success conflicting with your apparent idealism. Ketu in Dhanishta has already fought a war for spirituality and self-knowledge. Mars, the ruler of Dhanishta, also acts like Ketu so the influence of Ketu is more prominent here. Ketu, which represents both moksha and past lives, suggests that the achievements of Rahu in Magha are only due to the karma of the past. This recognition will make a more complete individual, but those who feel that they alone are responsible for their success are deluding themselves and not making use of the spiritual help that Ketu's dominance of this axis suggests.

The conflict between Magha and Shatabhishak
Shat means hundred and *Bhishak* means demons, so this nakshatra can be both demonic and godly. Both are sides of man, who has to conquer one to find the other. Ketu in Shatabhishak shows that in a past life the soul struggled with its own inadequacies.

This nakshatra axis reverses the rulership of Rahu Ketu. Rahu rules Shatabhishak where Ketu is now placed and Ketu rules Magha where Rahu is placed. The nodal axis creates confusion and lack of direction. In the past life Ketu in Shatabhishak had a difficult struggle dealing with its demons, and needs to connect to Rahu so that burden of those struggles can be relieved. Magha is in Leo ruled by the Sun and Shatabhishak in Aquarius ruled by Saturn, so it is important to see where the Sun and Saturn are placed in your natal chart. These two have a difficult relationship with each other but if they are well placed natally they can becoming temporary friends, allowing you to connect the past with the present and making this axis easier to experience.

Rahu in Purva Phalguni (13°20 to 26°40 Leo) and
Ketu in Shatabhishak (13°20 to 20°00 Aquarius) or
Purva Bhadra (20°00 to 26°40 Aquarius)

Rahu in Purva Phalguni will have Ketu placed in either Shatabhishak or Purva Bhadra. *Phal* means fruit and *Guni* connects to gunas (the three basic qualities), so Phalguni is the nakshatra which gives us the fruit of our good deeds. Purva means first, indicating it is the former part of the Phalguni nakshatras. This nakshatra has the capacity to fulfil our desires on a materialistic level but Rahu's placement here can work in two ways. It either enjoys the pleasures Purva Phalguni has to offer, or becomes relentlessly engaged in a search to find the perfect pleasures in life.

Venus, the ruler of Purva Phalguni, is a special friend to Rahu so the promise here is that Rahu will be fulfilled and able to enjoy the fruits of previous karma. If Rahu does not appreciate what it is receiving, these experiences will instead cause depression and disappointment.

The ruling deity of Purva Phalguni is Bhaga, the god of good fortune and luck, and indicates that the fruits of Purva Phalguni are usually highly auspicious. The Indian belief is that good luck shines on you because of the actions of your past life. Bhaga is a Sun god, one of the twelve sons of Aditi the universal mother, and Bhaga shines his solar radiance on this nakshatra endowing wealth, prosperity, affluence, luxuries and comforts. Rahu and the Sun have a karmic relationship as one darkens the other during an eclipse, but the Sun also exposes Rahu. This indicates the ability of Purva Phalguni to expose the good or bad points of Rahu – although as this is a lucky nakshatra it is more likely to expose the good side. Purva Phalguni's ruler is Venus, who is Rahu's guru and helps Rahu bring out its best. One of the important qualities of Venus is that it will allow you to make your own mistakes and help you along whatever path you wish to take. So if Rahu in Purva Phalguni wants to take a negative path, Venus as its ruler will help and not deter it. As Purva Phalguni is also the nakshatra of children, Rahu's placement here indicates children of the mind – in other words the fruits of our mental creativity.

The conflict between Purva Phalguni and Shatabhishak

Ketu in Shatabishak can have many meanings. The past life was connected to demons that we need to destroy within us, but *Abhishak* also means healers - so Shatabishak can mean 'a hundred healers'. It has special healing properties and brings with it the ability to use herbs for psychological disorders. Rahu, the ruler of Shatabhishak, created obstacles that were faced in previous lives, and now Ketu in Shatabhishak brings this knowledge to this life. It remembers the struggles to annihilate the ego, the work done in healing others and at times the heavy price paid in karmic terms. Ketu in Shatabhishak suggests a past life of sacrifice, as a result of which you are being given a break from the soul's spiritual journey to enjoy life in Purva Phalguni. However if the mind still hankers after the abstinence of the spiritual struggle, it may feel extremely guilty about the benefits that are given to enjoy now. The relationship between the two nakshatra rulers Venus and Rahu is excellent and the transference of knowledge from past to present should be easy. Those with Rahu in Purva Phalguni should take stock and enjoy what life has to offer. Keeping at the back of your mind the struggle it took to get this far will enable you to create good karma for the future.

The conflict between Purva Phalguni and Purva Bhadra

Ketu in Purva Bhadra shows a past life of idealism where the individual soul had the courage to change its course and discover the true meaning of life. Purva means first and Bhadra beautiful, so this is where the true beauty of an individual can emerge. Ketu gained this beauty of inner perfection in the past when the soul was at peace with itself leading a life with no expectation of glorification or personal reward. Now this beautiful soul has the final few opportunities to experience the pleasures in life.

Rahu in Purva Phalguni gets involved in creating new desires or struggling to fulfil existing ones and can therefore create more karma for itself. The conflict of this axis is to let go of the past and be comfortable in the present. Purva Bhadra's ruler Jupiter is inimical to Venus and therefore does not easily transmit the karmic path from Ketu to Rahu. The soul still feels it has a long journey to complete. It is important to remember that past life karma has completed most of the struggles and this life has many fruits to offer, if only you allow your mind to accept them.

Rahu in Uttara Phalguni (26°40 Leo to 10°00 Virgo) and Ketu in Purva Bhadra (26°40 Aquarius to 3°20 Pisces) or Uttara Bhadra (3°20 to 10°00 Pisces)

Rahu in Uttara Phalguni will have Ketu placed in either Purva Bhadra or Uttara Bhadra. Uttara Phalguni is the continuation of Purva Phalguni, the male energy to Purva's female. It represents the other half of the picture. Phalguni is the nakshatra which brings us the fruit of our good deeds in past lives, and Rahu here wants to experience all the good luck now. Uttara Phalguni is ruled by the Sun, its deity Aryaman is a sun god, so the solar energy dominates. The Sun signifies creation and carries within it the knowledge of individual karma. Uttara Phalguni allows the soul to recognise its own failings as well as understanding the restrictions imposed by the limited destiny of this life. The position of the Sun on your birth chart will indicate where Rahu is now taking you. The solar personality either glows radiantly or is eclipsed by shadows, and both are more of a possibility here than in any other placement of Rahu.

When Rahu in Uttara Phalguni starts to concentrate on its inner strength it develops the capacity to tolerate pain and slowly becomes strong. Phalguni suggests good fortune but Rahu recognises that the good fortune is linked to past karma, and herein lies the power. It no longer just accepts the material role but allows itself to develop as an individual and contribute to the positive karma of the future.

The conflict between Uttara Phalguni (Leo) and Purva Bhadra (Aq)
Ketu in Purva Bhadra connects the emergence of the inner beauty to a past life. The ruling deity of Purva Bhadra is Aja Ekapada which presides over the state of oneness with infinity, something Ketu has experienced in the past. It is like a still lake with many undercurrents that to the naked eye appears calm. Ketu links the soul to this profound energy which will bring memories for the individual that will make them yearn for a return to that life. The sacrifices in previous lives have created situations where we are now able to enjoy their fruits.

Ketu in Purva Bhadra suggests that the soul had almost reached its state of perfection in previous lives when it chose to be reborn to a comfortable material life. The soul struggles to accept these material rewards as it has to adjust again to become part of life's pains and pleasures. If Rahu is disconnected to Ketu's past life knowledge it will struggle immensely with its material goals, feeling guilty about its good fortune or fearing to lose it totally. Those with this axis must understand that now its journey to self-realisation is to experience and enjoy life. To express your material karma fruitfully is also a path towards moksha.

Uttara Phalguni is ruled by the Sun and placed in its own sign, allowing Rahu to bring out its best qualities. Ketu is in Purva Bhadra ruled by Jupiter and in the sign of Saturn. Jupiter and Saturn bring a balance between expansion and restriction and this shows that past life issues are much more complicated than the present. Rahu in Uttara Phalguni and Leo can struggle against power or bring out its hidden qualities. Ketu's controllers, Saturn and Jupiter, may create complexities related to the appropriate use of power. As Jupiter and the Sun are good friends they will communicate with each other, making it possible for these polarities to connect.

The conflict between Uttara Phalguni (Virgo) and Purva Bhadra (Pisces)
Rahu position in Uttara Phalguni and Virgo means it has to connect back to its karmic roots through service and duty to others. This will help to build discipline and preparation for the difficult spiritual task ahead. The comfort of Leo in Uttara Phalguni has now passed.

Ketu in Purva Bhadra represents the soul moving into a state of stillness. In comparison to Rahu's placement where the soul is learning about self control, Ketu in Pisces and Purva Bhadra has the soul giving up the right to control life, allowing greater forces to guide it. Rahu finds this difficult as its inclination is to analyse everything. The real insight comes when Rahu realises its inherent spirituality and accepts the work and service it has to undertake in this world.

The choice is now with the individual to live a life of a karma yogi (one who is happy with their material path) and lighten their burden of karma.

The conflict between Uttara Phalguni and Uttara Bhadra

Ketu in Uttara Bhadra is in Pisces, which ruled by Jupiter, but the nakshatra is ruled by Saturn. This combination brings an initial resistance but eventual harmony as Jupiter gives the wisdom to face adversity in the search for one's spiritual roots. Pisces is the end of the spiritual journey and Ketu in Uttara Bhadra indicates a past life where we almost completed this aim. A person may reach a time in their life where their consciousness merges into the dark night sky, where everything becomes as one. Then out of this mysterious darkness creativity emerges, like the day that breaks at the end of night.

The dawning of knowledge in the soul and its past life journey is reflected by Rahu in Uttara Phalguni. The soul in its physical life also recognises the need for the final journey to a beautiful place - a journey that was made in a past life. Saturn's rulership of Uttara Bhadra suggests that there is still some karma left before true enlightenment can be possible. The next step of the journey has to be taken by Rahu in Uttara Ashadha. The Saturn and Sun rulerships of these nakshatras suggest that the issues of darkness and light, death and re-birth, are intimately connected to this axis. Saturn is the son of the Sun from his shadow wife Chhayya; the Sun reflects the soul beginning its journey to find itself through the shadow planet, and the need to pay its karmic debt (Saturn) whenever it embarks on a journey to earth. The rebirth allows the soul to work out its karma and become stronger. The present has to be accepted regardless of the situation, and you should not feel guilty of your material requirements. There has been enough sacrifice. The more you work with your life now, the easier it will be for you.

Rahu in Hasta (10°00 to 23°20 Virgo) and
Ketu in Uttara Bhadra (10°00 to 16°40 Pisces) or
Revati (16°40 to 23°20 Pisces)

Rahu in Hasta will have Ketu placed in either Uttara Bhadra or Revati. Hasta is placed entirely in the sign of Virgo ruled by Mercury and the nakshatra is ruled by the Moon. This may result in the logical, rational part of the brain restricting the searching, more spiritual qualities in the individual, or vice versa. *Hasta* means hand, which reflects an individual's destiny and represents the individual effort. Rahu placed in Hasta emphasises the attempts of man to try to control his destiny through his own efforts. The intuitive Moon allows a look beyond the ties of the material world, but Rahu's placement in the intellectual part of Hasta can restrict the spiritual growth through fear and mistrust. The essence of Rahu in Hasta lies in the karmic relationship between the Moon and Rahu; at the time of a lunar eclipse Rahu's shadow becomes visible, indicating that the Moon-ruled nakshatras can expose the truth about the node. If Rahu allows itself to look beyond the inner darkness, it can see the light that leads to the path of enlightenment.

Hasta provides immense opportunities for an individual to change and grow. The inner urge is to stride ahead but external forces may restrict causing conflict. Souls are guided to the path of renunciation and public service, and many become leaders of a renewing and sustaining power in the community. Rahu in Hasta experiences different types of continued personal growth – to find fulfilment it needs to find its spiritual essence.

The conflict between Uttara Bhadra and Hasta
Ketu in Uttara Bhadra shows a past life where the individual let go of their fears and moved into the final journey towards the maturity of the soul. Saturn's rulership shows the heavy price that was paid in finally annihilating the individual identification. Uttara Bhadra's deity is Ahir Budhnya, which is linked to Soma (the Moon) and is associated with water and darkness; the passivity of darkness is the mysterious source from which all forms of creation have arisen. Ahir Budhnya is also a serpent that represents wisdom - the snake's shedding of its skin symbolises re-birth and the cycles of life that a soul must experience. (See Ashlesha nakshatra).

Ketu in Uttara Bhadra is stripped bare of all artifice and this creates extreme sensitivity within. You come into this life with a poor self-image, so Rahu in Hasta is always trying to justify its personality. It can be over confident on the outside and fearful and vulnerable within. As Ketu is ruled by Saturn and Rahu by the Moon, this relationship can create blocks which make it tough for the past life information to filter through. Trying to seek the calmness from their previous lives, Saturn and Ketu will feel Rahu's efforts in this world are of no use. It can make you struggle against unseen forces when the main opposition is yourself. Try to stop controlling your life through intellectual analysis and allow yourself to trust and use your intuitive power.

The conflict between Hasta and Revati
Revati is the last nakshatra of the zodiac and is powerful in realising the ultimate truths about life, death, transformation and change. The celestial messenger Mercury rules Revati and it is in Revati that you sow the seeds for fruition at a later date. It signifies endings and beginnings. Revati also means abundant or wealthy. With Ketu placed there, spiritual wealth was acquired in a past life

and the soul now comes into a final incarnation to experience the restrictions of a material life.

This axis is important as the soul has experienced one cycle of soul growth and is about to embark on the next one. Rahu can help with the change and transformation demanded by Hasta, and the spiritual wealth of the past life can be a stepping stone to the new maturity of the soul. The struggle of Hasta and Revati is within the mind of an individual as it sets up barriers to spiritual growth, yet if we allow ourselves to relax and believe in our intuitive power, we are able to go beyond the normal expectations.

Rahu in Chitra (23°20 Virgo to 6°40 Libra) and Ketu in Revati (23°20 to 30°00 Pisces) or Ketu in Ashwini (0°00 to 6°40 Aries)

Rahu in Chitra will have Ketu placed in either Revati or Ashwini. *Chitra* means a reflection or a beautiful picture, and it reflects the potential of the soul. The Chitra individual has two types of life experience: one which is almost unaware of its spiritual potential, and the other where circumstances and situations force the individual to recognise their higher nature. The personality is reformed but the process is painful as the ego has to be cut away in order for the inner soul to emerge. Rahu in Chitra reinforces its illusionary quality – which is most profound in this nakshatra. The illusions and shadows that Rahu represents are so strong that you can easily live in a false or unrealistic world. This can still allow you to be successful yet you will feel unfulfilled until the soul connection is made.

The conflict between Chitra and Revati

Revati's ruling deity is Pushan, a solar god. Pushan rules the auspicious time of the Sun's death and rebirth. Its rulership of Revati connects to the dawn, which carries within it the promise of light and beginning. Ketu shows a past life where the soul experienced the stillness that forms the ending of one cycle of manifestation. A soul completing one cycle of maturity does not mean it has gained full enlightenment, but it understands that one part of the soul's journey has ended and a new one begun. This is reflected onto Rahu in Chitra, which is immersed in matter. Chitra has a hard crust formed by life's experiences, but this crust will break at some time during the individual's lifetime when it will stop reflecting illusion and become a true mirror of the soul. Chitra is ruled by Mars, and Revati by Mercury, two planets that are extremely inimical to each other. Mars is the planet of action and Mercury the intellect, but in this axis they have to see the other side of their personalities. Mercury is the celestial messenger carrying messages from the gods to earthlings and Mars is the spiritual warrior who has the courage to undertake the spiritual journey. When the crust of Chitra breaks open Mars will show its courage and understand that life's lessons must now be expressed. The strengths of Mars and Mercury and their relative positions to each other in your chart will explain what can be done.

The conflict between Chitra and Ashwini
Ketu is placed in its own nakshatra, Ashwini, in the sign of Aries. Ashwini indicates the beginning of the soul's journey into earthly life and Ketu is a mystical power indicating the soul at the beginning of its search for moksha. This combination led to entanglement in a karmic web - the soul started enjoying life and slowly lost its inherent purity in the world of illusion.

This is a conflict between the spiritual and material levels. Ketu in Ashwini is extremely idealistic and attached to past life experience. Mars, as its ruler, also governs Chitra where Rahu is placed. Rahu thinks that life is full of materialistic achievements, and either ignores or is disconnected to its spiritual self. So Rahu in Chitra leads to the individual experiencing some kind of traumatic life situation that makes them aware of their inner soul. This will create a connection to its past life and the real search of the soul begins.

Rahu in Swati (6°40 to 20°00 Libra) and
Ketu in Ashwini (6°40 to 13°20 Aries) or
Bharani (13°20 to 20°00 Aries)

Rahu in Swati will have Ketu placed in either Ashwini or Bharani. Swati indicates the depth of the soul's involvement in materialism. It means a sword, and Rahu uses Swati as a tool for self-advancement, cutting through any competition and obstacles in its path. Like a sword it can be used negatively or positively. This is a powerful position but a person should be aware that it can make for an obsessive personality. The individual may recognise no failure, yet be unhappy with the success he achieves.

Rahu is in its own nakshatra but feels dissatisfied with life. If it gratifies this dissatisfaction with more material achievement it can bring an emptiness and lack of pleasure to the accomplishments. Rahu often teaches life lessons through satiation, as this will eventually lead the individual towards change. Swati will move towards the spiritual meaning of life only after the other urges have been fulfilled.

The conflict between Swati and Ashwini
Ketu is in its own nakshatra in Ashwini, which is named after the Ashwins, the twin sons of the sun god. The Sun is meant to represent the parent - the divine link of the Sun to the first nakshatra means that there is an important

evolutionary process taking place here. Ketu is said to eclipse the Sun but it is the Sun that helps give energy to the whole process taking place. Ketu's position indicates a past life where the soul took its first steps into the earthly domain, and then became eclipsed as it embraced the new dawn of light.

Rahu is also placed in its own nakshatra so this is a powerful nodal axis. Vedic astrology considers that Rahu Ketu placed in their own axis can be difficult because the polarity struggle is intensified. Usually Rahu and Ketu adopt the influence of the planetary ruler of the nakshatra in which they are placed, and that can create a lightness and an understanding of the karmic issues. But both Rahu and Ketu in their own nakshatras are very intense. You feel surrounded by shadows, and trying to understand the self and gain the right insight can be difficult. There was idealism and faith in a previous life but now this may be reflected back from Swati as distrust and disappointment. On a soul level the Swati Ashwini axis is one of cynicism and idealism, but even though Rahu in Swati is immersed in materialism it stands the chance of regaining its innocence and finding its way back to the source.

The conflict between Swati and Bharani
Ketu is in Bharani and ruled by Venus. *Bharani* means to cherish, support and nourish, and it expresses feminine energy in its pure form. The basic principle of this nakshatra is Shakti, the passive female power which has an important place in vedic philosophy. This energy incubates the soul and transports it from one realm of existence to another. Put another way, it takes you from a spiritual manifestation to a more objective one. Ketu in Bharani means that the past life was spent in playing a supporting role, nourishing others and allowing the soul to develop on earth. But Ketu in Bharani can reject your present need for passion and sensuality.

Swati is the name of the wife of the Sun god, so in Swati the Sun forgets its spiritual purpose and becomes involved in the pleasures and pains of relationship. For the moment it is not bothered about moksha or enlightenment. Ketu in Bharani shows a past life where sexual expression was the key and this axis can be obsessive over issues of sex and relationships. Rahu needs to experience satiation and Ketu teaches rejection so the wheel of experience is all connected to relationships here.

**Rahu in Vishakha (20⁰00 Libra to 3⁰20 Scorpio) and
Ketu in Bharani (20⁰00 to 26⁰40 Aries) or
Krittika (26⁰40 Aries to 3⁰20 Taurus)**

Rahu in Vishakha will have Ketu placed in either Bharani or Krittika. Rahu in Vishakha is at the stage where an individual forces himself to look within and learn from previous experiences. The soul is standing at the threshold of higher experiences and is able to take on board new lessons. The change does not take place without a great churning of emotions. A unique feature of this nakshatras is non-attraction, a special type of dissatisfaction with existing conditions and Rahu intensifies the restlessness and psychological turmoil raging within.

Vishakha is the only nakshatra ruled by two deities - the two main Vedic gods, Agni and Indra. Agni, the sacred fire, represents penance and Indra sensuous enjoyments, so these two can cause much conflict in the mind of Vishakha. Rahu placed here creates a sense of dissatisfaction with both the material and the spiritual sides of life, for it will first experience sensuality to the extreme with romance and sexual adventures, then when these pursuits lose their satisfaction it moves into the spiritual aspect. Agni burns away the negative sheaths connected to materialistic enjoyment and the individual becomes extremely spiritual, shunning their earlier life. Rahu in Vishakha is a life experienced on the threshold. The soul is still committed to materialistic enjoyment yet stands at the door of spiritual development. The unhappiness lies in trying to adopt one at the expense of the other.

The conflict between Vishakha and Bharani

Ketu is in Bharani so the past life could have been one of excess. Bharani is basically feminine and allows itself to be a receptacle for the seed of humanity, which in this case was planted in a past life. There is a darker side to its nature, symbolised by the god Yama, who rules darkness. Ketu in Bharani suggests that by agreeing to carry this seed in the past, it became controlled by the laws of dath and rebirth imposed by Yama. Bharani brings this aspect into the present life, which impacts on the sexuality of the individual.

Rahu in Vishakha may make its search through sexual adventure and promiscuity, especially at a younger age. Ketu in Bharani is connected to sexuality too, yet as a moksha planet it is uncomfortable having to work through sexual issues. Ketu can reject sexuality and placed in Bharani may foster a feeling of sexual inadequacy. This could manifest simply as an inability to express one's sensuous side, or there may more negative energies. Rahu tries to overcome the sexual issues by ignoring its past life and trying to sort out problems through new experiences. In order to align this axis it is important not just to identify life with sexual happiness. Swati is in the sign of Venus which rules Bharani, so the answer lies in bringing awareness to your relationships with others. Rejecting partners or pursuing multiple partnerships is not the solution. Staying with a partner who can fill the void within you, is the best way to resolve this axis.

The conflict between Vishakha (Libra) and Krittika (Aries)
Ketu in Krittika is ruled by the Sun, but Krittika itself is passive. It has both constructive and destructive principles and shows that in the past we were born into a life where the soul had a choice of how it was going to develop. The strength and placement of the Sun will indicate how you used this energy. Ketu placed here is in the nakshatra of its arch enemy - the Sun. But the Sun is also exalted in a Ketu nakshatra, revealing the soul's desire. In other words Rahu in Vishakha will bring you the true experience of the seeds sown in a previous life. Rahu must also take heed of its zodiac position in Libra and balance the two opposing energies that Vishakha brings as the present life experience. The real issue is: what is Ketu bringing into this life? The placements of the Sun and Mars are extremely important here because if they are situated in difficult houses or positions to each other there will be a lot of past life baggage. Jupiter as the ruler of Vishakha will be eager to transfer the Krittika experience to this life and harvest its fruit, so much depends on how you handled things in the past.

The conflict between Vishakha (Scorpio) and Krittika (Taurus)
Rahu in Vishakha and Scorpio should avoid the tendency to self-destruct. It is obsessed either with its spiritual pursuits or with its sensual nature. Rahu in Vishakha can awaken the kundalini too, quickly creating fears and bringing forward the negative aspects of past lives. Ketu placed in Krittika Taurus will feel uncomfortable with its inherent materialism, seeing this as the result of wrong choices made in previous lives. The challenge of this axis is to create positive results from past life experiences - but the key is discipline and a belief in the goodness of your own nature. As the relationship between the nakshatra rulers Jupiter and the Sun is good, the end result will be positive.

Rahu in Anuradha (3°20 to 16°40 Scorpio) and
Ketu in Krittika (3°20 to 10°00 Taurus) or
Ketu in Rohini (10°00 to 16°40) Taurus)

Rahu in Anuradha will have Ketu placed in either Krittika or Rohini. Anuradha as a tiny spark makes us aware of our divine connection. Anuradha usually reveals hidden purity but Rahu placed here does not often recognise this. Saturn's rulership of Anuradha shows that many karmic responsibilities have to be faced now. The revelation eventually takes place when Anuradha cuts through the illusion of materialism to reveal the latent potential that was previously hidden. The Anuradha approach is idealistic and its aim divine, helping us get rid of our darkness and gives us light in return. By contrast the Rahu approach is usually demonic and the aim materialistic, but Saturn teaches Rahu to control its forces and channel them more positively.

The conflict between Anuradha and Krittika
Ketu is in the nakshatra of its arch enemy the Sun and is unhappy with the materialistic aims of Taurus. Ketu is a mendicant and the Sun a king. Ketu believes in giving away power and breaking bonds with everything material, while the Sun is power, and controls all life. This inner conflict, reflected by Ketu in Krittika, is what you bring into this life. The real issues of Ketu in Krittika have to be understood, but there is still a sense of immense dissatisfaction with the affairs of the past. Ketu in Krittika suggests that you did not come to terms with the karma of your past life so there is a sense of restlessness and disquiet within.

The crisis of this nakshatra axis is that both nodes are in their debilitated positions so forced to work against their basic nature. In Anuradha, Rahu learns about giving up desires, while in Krittika, Ketu learns to cope with materialism. Anuradha is a moksha nakshatra seeking divine love while Krittika is a nakshatra that craves power and making its impact on the world. Yet in their hidden psyche both Rahu and Ketu have the tools to work against their natures to become part of a whole. The position of Saturn and the Sun in the natal chart will indicate how well you are able to realise answers from what is a difficult starting position.

The conflict between Rohini and Anuradha
Rohini in Sanskrit means red, which relates to passion and sensuality. The inner core of Rohini is full of emotions, romanticism and love. Rohini has lots of love to give and seeks a partner through with whom it can find the ultimate answers to life. Ketu in Rohini wants to reject love and be ascetic so it is extremely uncomfortable with Rohini's passionate nature. Yet Rohini's aim is for moksha, the same as Ketu, it is only the way of expression that differs. Ketu will feel debilitated in Rohini, indicating a past life of luxury and pleasure that the soul was never at ease with. If Ketu understands that beneath all the outer pomp and passion there is the same idealism that it needs, it will not feel so uncomfortable.

Because the Moon rules Rohini and Saturn rules Anuradha, the relationship is not an easy one and it illustrates the difficulties in transmitting soul lessons from one end of the axis to the other. Both the nodes are placed in positions of crisis so they have to find a different way of expressing themselves. Rahu in Anuradha has to move from materialism to spirituality, while the conflict Ketu faced in a past life should be put in perspective and not allowed to control your happiness now.

Rahu in Jyeshta (16°40 to 23°40 Scorpio) and Ketu in Rohini (16°40 to 23°40 Taurus) or Mrigasira (23°40 to 30°00 Taurus)

Rahu in Jyeshta will have Ketu placed in either Rohini or Mrigasira. Jyeshta is an extremely powerful nakshatra because here the soul breaks away from its materialistic course and moves towards the final part of the journey. Jyeshta gives a person a strong sense of destiny and a struggle with the lower and higher desires. The ruler of Jyeshta is Mercury, the celestial link between materialism and spiritualism. Rahu in Jyeshta is at a critical point because it is debilitated and is likely to take you into the non-spiritual world of desire which Indra, the deity of Jyeshta, represents. Indra had the capacity to control its desires however, so Rahu in Jyeshta may feel it can experience any type of desire and be in control of it. This is a mistake because there must be discipline and a careful nurturing of your life direction. If you go too far along the wrong path it can be difficult to retrace your steps. Jyeshta is connected to the kundalini which gives immense powers when energised. For the kundalini to unfold in the correct way you need go beyond the attachments of the physical world. Once this discipline is achieved there is the possibility of communicating with spirits and the knowledge of past and future lives. This is the potential contained within Jyeshta, but Rahu in Jyeshta can be too impatient to activate this kundalini power. Its natural curiosity may lead it to unleash the kundalini before it is ready and when this happens it rises like an enraged serpent creating all types of psychological problems. If you have this Rahu placement it is important to go into new spiritual disciplines carefully. Prepare yourself through yoga and other spiritual practices until you feel mentally strong enough to explore this side of your nature.

The conflict between Jyeshta and Rohini
Rohini is ruled by the Moon so Ketu in Rohini shows a past life where emotional need was dominant. Ketu in debilitation is forced to go against it natural instincts and this can bring a psychological disenchantment with love and relationships. Rohini transports the soul from the spiritual to the material but Ketu wants to go in the opposite direction.

This axis shows a struggle with desire. Ketu in Rohini rejects all the passion and sensuality that Rahu in Jyeshta feels it must experience. Rahu has to learn that after it has satiated its desires it must assume a control over them. Ketu in Rohini should avoid bringing past life emotional issues into this life as they are hindering its growth. Its emotional crisis point was in the past.

The conflict between Jyeshta and Mrigasira
Mriga means a deer and *Sira* means head. The head of the deer is a symbol of

the Moon but this nakshatra is also ruled by Mars - the planet of action and adventure. Mrigasira is considered the birth place of the intellect, so Mars allows us to be intellectually as well as physically adventurous here. Ketu in Mrigasira shows a past life where an intellectual search into the realities of life began and, as Ketu acts like Mars, the identification was of an intellectual warrior. However Ketu was very uncomfortable when it realised that the search in the outer world was encasing the soul into material life.

This is a very profound position for the nodal axis with an opportunity for the soul to give it up its material entanglements and move towards self-realisation. Mrigasira Mars once went into areas of life without considering the consequences and created desires that tied them to the materialistic life. Jyeshta Mercury will have a life of polarities: the need to gratify sensuality and the need to explore spirituality. As the rulers of the nakshatras (Mars and Mercury) are inimical to each other it will be difficult to connect the past to the present and use the knowledge gathered in previous lives. But if you can look beyond your desires and material needs you will slowly recover your inner knowledge.

If Rahu is in the last pada of Jyeshta (26°40 to 30°00 Scorpio), it will be in gandanta, showing the potential for deep spiritual experiences. Life is tied to an emotional knot that can become tighter and tighter creating fear and worry, but if you take the power of your life experiences and work with patience to unravel the spiritual knots, you can achieve success.

Rahu in Mula (0°00 to 13°20 Sagittarius) and Ketu in Mrigasira (0°00 to 6°40 Gemini) or Ardra (6°40 to 13°20 Gemini)

Rahu in Mula will have Ketu placed in either Mrigasira or Ardra. Rahu in Mula is ruled by Ketu, making this is a power point of the nakshatra system. Mula is the root from which all humanity flowers and Rahu placed here has to learn to let go of the more basic human needs and start to reach upwards. If you feel disillusioned with life and its prospects, maybe you are looking for happiness in the wrong place. Rahu in Mula will only be truly fulfilled when it starts to look upward.

The conflict between Mula and Mrigasira
Mrigasira marks the beginning of an intellectual search, and Ketu in Mrigasira suggests a past life where intellect, reasoning and mental pursuits dominated. Nothing was taken at face value without proper analysis, but this may have created problems as the more you questioned the less you knew. Mrigasira is a profound nakshatra where purity and impurity meet and the soul is brought into contact with materialism. As a moksha planet Ketu is unhappy with the

search for truth through material means, and this may bring unhappiness.

Ketu in Mrigasira is connected to the deity Soma - another name for the Moon. Soma also links Ketu and the past life to an intellectual analytical search. Now Rahu in Mula has the responsibility to stop that search, cut away from the material desires and force the mind and soul towards its next journey. The problems of the Mula Mrigasira axis are rooted in the past life, so understanding the lessons it brought will enable you to move on. You will need to study the position of Mars to Ketu in your chart to throw more light on this.

The conflict between of Mula and Ardra

The crisis of the Mula Ardra axis can appear to be a 'Catch 22' situation. The past represents the future and the future - the past. Those with this axis need to sit back, slow down and take stock of their spiritual confusion through a practice of yoga or meditation. The need for kriyamana karma or the new karma we create from past experiences is strong, for the soul feels it is searching through mist and shadows as aspects of our lives are obscured. When you look to the past to guide you, it points you towards the future, yet the future points back to the past. If you are reading this you are already on the path of understanding, so think of yourself as the seed that will burst from the pod to form a beautiful tree that grows heavenward. The position of Jupiter and Mercury on your chart will also indicate how this process can develop.

Rahu in Purva Ashadha (13°20 to 26°40 Sagittarius)
Ketu in Ardra (13°20 to 20°00 Gemini) or
Punarvasu (20°00 to 26°40 Gemini)

Rahu in Purva Ashadha will have Ketu in either Ardra or Punarvasu. Purva Ashadha means that which cannot be suppressed, and Rahu placed here will staunchly pursue life to find out its true nature. This is a Venus-ruled nakshatra and Venus is the spiritual teacher who advises the demons, including Rahu, so the this will enable Rahu to lead us towards finding our own light. Purva Ashadha develops knowledge and wisdom through life experiences that can never be taken away. The meaning of life can be suddenly revealed, hidden knowledge uncovered and the intuitive faculties sharpened. There were difficulties in a previous life but now is the opportunity to turn dissatisfaction into happiness. Rahu in Purva Ashadha is searching moksha and self-realisation.

The conflict between Purva Ashadha and Ardra

Ardra means green and moist, and it is ruled by Rahu which aspires to the highest ambitions. Ardra's sphere of activity is connected to the mind, so Ketu in Ardra shows a past life where most of its answers still lay in the future. This created a frustration in the psyche as it was unsure what the future demanded. The main conflict of Purva Ashadha and Ardra is about trying to live in the present. Rahu is in Purva Ashadha but it also rules Ketu in Ardra; Ketu will fight for dominance yet its questions can only be answered through Rahu. The best way to resolve this crisis is by working in the present. Purva Ashadha is ruled by Venus, which will help you to achieve what you want for yourself want for yourself - it will not force you into areas of which you have no awareness. Purva Ashadha is a very changeable nakshatra and can create difficulties by looking for new ideas and perspectives, but Venus creates the best situations to use past life talents. Do not feel uncomfortable with it, just remember all this is leading you towards more personal knowledge.

The conflict between Purva Ashadha and Punarvasu
Punarvasu deals with the transfer of knowledge from the spiritual to the earthly plane, and Jupiter, the true teacher, has the responsibility of guiding this process. Punarvasu deals with the wandering mind in search of its true identity, so Ketu in Punarvasu shows a person who spent his past life searching for this. Purva Ashadha is ruled by Venus and Punarvasu is ruled by Jupiter. Both these planets are vedic gurus but with responsibilities to teach different sides of life and their rulerships can create conflict. Rahu ruled by Venus is comfortable with the present yet may be unaware of a past life connection if Jupiter does not allow this to happen. The role of Jupiter and Venus in this axis is important as they do not naturally allow the invisible connection between Rahu and Ketu to take place. Both nakshatras are trying to find answers but they may leave you searching on two different levels and never find the connection between past and present.

**Rahu in Uttara Ashadha (26°40 Sagittarius to 10°00 Capricorn) and
Ketu in Punarvasu (26°40 Gemini to 3°20 Cancer) or
Pushya (3°20 to 10°00 Cancer)**

Rahu in Uttara Ashadha will have Ketu placed in either Punarvasu or Pushya. In Purva Ashadha (the preceding Rahu nakshatra), there were the beginnings of psychological changes, but their assimilation takes place in Uttara Ashadha. Rahu can unveil hidden powers but the individual will go through some difficulties before experiencing them. The first problem is the relationship between the Sun and Rahu. This relationship of darkness and light becomes the fundamental issue of Rahu in Uttara Ashadha. What you fear the most has the ability to bring the maximum light. Those with Rahu here can lead a life unaware of their own light, then a dramatic event forces them to confront their fears and bring out their true colours.

Uttara Ashadha itself is ruled by the Sun and Rahu in Uttara Ashadha is in Capricorn ruled by Saturn. Consciousness is signified by the Sun but the influence of Saturn and Rahu move things in a different direction. Saturn teaches knowledge through experience, Capricorn encourages the individual to cooperate with the divine plan, and Rahu helps Saturn fulfil its duty. Discipline, hard work and responsibility for one's karma are the important issues here.

The conflict between Uttara Ashadha (Sag) and Punarvasu (Gemini)
Punarvasu is the universal mother who cares for all. Ketu deals with past life impressions and in Punarvasu it had to experience rejection of love in some way. Now there may be a problem with the ability to give and receive love as Ketu in Punarvasu tries to find the correct surroundings to express its soul properly.

The psychological conflict of Ketu in Punarvasu is transferred to Rahu in Uttara Ashadha more easily here than in the previous axis, because Jupiter and the Sun are friends. However this transference of knowledge does not ease the conflict of the axis. The sign dispositor of Uttara Ashadha is Sagittarius and the nakshatra dispositor of Ketu is Jupiter, so Rahu is influenced both by Jupiter and past life issues. The rejection of love in a past life makes Rahu in Uttara Ashadha feel immensely lonely. To try and fill the emptiness Rahu in Uttara Ashadha searches relentlessly for love and emotion yet will intellectually reject them. As the answer to this axis lies with Ketu, it is important to realise that rejection is an issue brought in from previous lives and is not valid now. Learning to love ourselves and our spiritual heritage will gradually bring a change towards awareness, peace and happiness.

The conflict between Uttara Ashadha (Cap) and Punarvasu (Cancer)
The conflict of this axis is the transfer of power. Ketu in Punarvasu indicates a past life at the edge of new experiences and Rahu in Uttara Ashadha also stands at a threshold. Both deal with the mind and soul and how they change with life's experiences. Ketu in Punarvasu tries to block the individual's emotional needs while it lives life in different hues, letting go of the spiritual to experience the material. Meanwhile Rahu, representing the present life, has to take responsibility for all the past life experiences and karmas. Capricorn and Saturn are relentless in facing up to karmic debt and the Sun will burn away the wasteful experiences. It needs emotional and personal strength to master this axis for there can be fear and unhappiness if you do not understand your personal responsibility. The relationship between the two nakshatra rulers (Jupiter and the Sun) is a good one, so Ketu will connect to Rahu. This can either create a feeling of touching infinity or increase the fear and distrust. The position of Jupiter and the Sun will throw further light on how this process will happen.

The conflict between Uttara Ashadha and Pushya

Pushya works to nourish others and create conditions so that the world can thrive. The ruler of the Pushya is Saturn, but the nakshatra is placed in Cancer, which is ruled by the Moon. The connection of Saturn to the Moon shows that this life will have a profound impact on the mind. Pushya usually has no idea of its own beauty as it tends to work for others taking a long time to recognise the validity of past lives. Its difficulty in connecting emotionally makes the mind distance itself from its feelings. There is a fear of rejection and losing the emotional equilibrium for which you paid a heavy price in a past life.

Saturn and its connection to the luminaries dominate in this nakshatra. It is a challenge because the Sun and Moon are the lights of our life and Saturn is connected to Yama, the dark god of death. Rahu Ketu now become involved in this profound process of recognising the true needs of the soul and taking responsibility for past life actions. Love, affection and relationships become lessons from which the true needs are learned. Release your fears, let go of the personal ego and awaken your sleeping soul; you will find a different kind of love illuminating your life and Rahu will take you to your chosen Path. The quality of Saturn, Sun and Moon in your chart will indicate how intense your experience will be.

**Rahu in Shravana (10°00 to 23°20 Capricorn) and
Ketu in Pushya (10°00 to 16°40 Cancer) or
Ashlesha (16°40 to 23°20 Cancer)**

Rahu in Shravana will have Ketu placed in either Pushya or Ashlesha. *Shravana* means silence and Rahu in Shravana searches for silence amongst the frenzied activity of life. The ruler of this nakshatra is the Moon, signifying a mind which is forever vacillating, but here the mind has to learn the lesson of equilibrium and peace. Our earthly instincts must also be regulated to give us a deeper understanding of the essence of life. Rahu and the Moon have a difficult relationship because Rahu can exacerbate any fears. Shravana is an artha nakshatra, which indicates that life must be lived on practical terms, yet the focus of life has to be towards the spiritual. Rahu has to make sense of this ever changing perspective and bring a steadiness and grounding to its search. The need is for quietness and reflection now, even though Rahu finds it difficult to sit still for long enough to hear the sounds of silence. Saturn also puts a burden on the emotions, forcing us to take responsibility for our lives, which includes a slow leaning towards inward meditation. Rahu gradually learns to experience the silence of the soul and control its restlessness.

The conflict between Shravana and Pushya

Ketu in Pushya was frustrated by the limited destiny of the past life. Saturn brought some heavy burdens, and there was a need to fulfill the material potential of the soul so Ketu found it difficult to enjoy the pleasures that life had to offer. Ketu in Pushya now tries to come to terms with its materialistic past but brings a difficult Moon-Saturn psychology to the axis. The rejection of materialism yet the inability to ignore it, becomes a tough dilemma for Ketu and Pushya. The right way of recognising this past life lesson is to accept that the soul had to make difficult choices which may not have been true to its idealistic ambitions, yet that path is considered to be as spiritual as the other.

Rahu is in Shravana, ruled by the Moon, and in a sign ruled by Saturn. Ketu is placed in Pushya, ruled by Saturn and placed in the sign of the Moon. Ketu creates emotional and mental issues that have no connection to the present. But the individual must make an important transformation to a different level of consciousness and before that can happen old ideas must go and difficult karma must be faced. This axis challenges you to strengthen your mind, so meditation, yoga and following the right karmic path are important.

The conflict between Shravana and Ashlesha

Ashlesha means to embrace and indicates the soul fully embracing life so it can act out its karma. Ketu in Ashlesha, which is ruled by rational Mercury, suggests that while Ketu reasoned in the past to accept earthly constraints, part of it remained extremely dissatisfied with its compromise. Ketu now brings this inner dissatisfaction forward.

Ketu is in a Mercury nakshatra but Rahu is in a Moon one suggesting that the real crisis between Shravana and Ashlesha is the conflict between rationality and intuition - which one do you trust? Mercury is inimical to the Moon, so Ketu will not be helpful to Rahu in passing on its experiences. This can make the axis work independently creating mental conflict. The trust has to be put in the intuitive power as Rahu deals directly with this life experience.

Rahu in Dhanishta (23°20 Capricorn to 6°40 Aquarius) and Ketu in Ashlesha (23°20 to 30°00 Cancer) or Magha (0°00 to 6°40 Leo)

Rahu in Dhanishta will have Ketu in either Ashlesha or Magha. *Dhanishta* means wealthy in spirit and mind, and Rahu in Dhanishta shows a soul that recognises its darkness yet aspires towards superior wealth. This usually begins as a search for material wealth, but when that does not bring happiness the search becomes higher. The soul then begins an inner cleansing, facing its demons and preparing the ground for divine aspirations. Dhanishta, which is ruled by Mars, is placed in either Capricorn or Aquarius, both of which are ruled by Saturn. Mars and Saturn are opposing energies and Saturn will restrict the impulsiveness of Mars to break through spiritual barriers until the necessary karma has been faced.

Rahu in Dhanishta begins with an expanded ego, searching for enlightenment through achievements. But while a person is full of self-importance the Dhanishta lesson cannot be learnt. The Mars-Saturn combination that rules Rahu will cause conflict unless the individual can realise their inner strength and let go of the fears that control them.

The conflict between Dhanishta and Ashlesha

Ashlesha is linked to the snake. Its presiding deity is the Nagas, the Sanskrit name for the snake, and this symbolism of the celestial serpent means that Ketu in Ashlesha implies a major psychological transformation. Ashlesha is also ruled by the heavenly messenger Mercury so it has the ability to transmit information from the celestial to the material. Ketu is at a crossroads here as the past life was full of analysing these choices. There would have been some painful shedding of skins and little peace as the soul still had some distance to go. Ketu placed in the end degrees of Ashlesha will be placed at a gandanta point, the karmic knot that is difficult to unravel. Traumatic experiences from a past life will come into this one. This tough placementcan be handled with meditation and spiritual discipline. (See Remedial Measures).

The past life search in Ashlesha, where the soul found itself restricted by the laws of material life, are now being given the opportunity to flower in Dhanishta. The problem lies with Mercury and Mars, who are inimical to each other. Ketu in Ashlesha has a fund of knowledge that is not readily available to Rahu in Dhanishta. Mars and Rahu will try to conquer the world materially and remain unconscious of their higher nature, yet the soul is mature at this stage. If it recognises the more divine energies instead of the fear, it can direct the intellectual search to a more physical one, making the connection complete.

The conflict between Dhanishta and Magha

Ketu is in its own nakshatra in Magha and shows a past life committed to tamas, the material way of life which is illusion, darkness and attachment. Ketu, the significator of spiritual realisation, indicates the importance of experiencing the realities of life in order to fulfil the divine mission of the soul. Magha means 'mighty' or 'great' and the past life reveals an aspiration towards eminence. But Ketu in its own nakshatra intensifies the past life experiences, and Magha is in the sign of the Sun, so the aspiration for greatness could have grown out of hand leading to an overblown belief in one's own immortality. In Dhanishta however the soul learns to give up its ego. The axis transfers easily from Ketu to Rahu as Dhanishta is ruled by the Sun's friend Mars, which has a great belief in its own invincibility but this craving for power creates problems. Only by letting go of the personal identification and allowing yourself to work for others helps break the mould. You were successful in another life and have the power to be even more successful now - it is just the definition of success that has changed.

Rahu in Shatabhishak (6°40 to 20°00 Aquarius) and Ketu in Magha (6°40 to 13°20 Leo) or Ketu in Purva Phalguni (13°20 to 20°00 Leo)

Rahu in Shatabhishak will have Ketu placed in either Magha or Purva Phalguni. As Rahu progresses into the later nakshatras its power intensifies. Shatabhishak is placed in Aquarius, ruled by Saturn, and Rahu gives results like Saturn but on the psychological level. In Shatabhishak, Rahu impacts on the mind and creates spiritual blocks towards inner growth. *Shat* means hundred and *bhishak* means demons or healers, so it can be both demonic and godly, indicating both sides of human nature that have to be conquered. Rahu in Shatabhishak can be very secretive and private, always fighting hidden enemies, without realising that their dark nature is part of the process.

The greatest gurus and teachers are the ones who have emerged after conquering the darkness that surrounded them. This inner fight does not subside easily and can become a life-long struggle but it helps to bring the soul to maturity and ultimate enlightenment.

The conflict between Shatabhishak and Magha

Ketu in Magha is in its own nakshatra, achieving success yet remaining unattached to it. There is a rejection of the successful work achieved in a previous life and this can give a distorted sense of importance in the present. Ketu in Magha wanted the impossible - to achieve moksha while living a totally practical life and there were inevitably disappointments. As Magha is placed in Leo it is ruled by the Sun and so it is confused over issues connected to power and self. The conflict between Shatabhishak and Magha is about darkness and light.

The nodes are in their own nakshatras and Rahu has to come face to face with its karma from past lives. The negative and the positive have to be separated and processed. In Shatabhishak the soul has the choice of finding the hundred demons or the hundred healers. In my view, Rahu in Shatabhishak will always contact the demons first, but if it understands its true karmic responsibility it is then able to connect to the healing side. Saturn, as Rahu's sign ruler, will not allow further progress in life without paying the karmic debts and Ketu in Magha intensifies the debt of ego, individuality and personality. This is a profound position - the most complex of the whole axis - and it needs time to be understood. The crisis it represents in life can be controlled by some spiritual work on your part.

The conflict between Shatabhishak and Purva Phalguni
Ketu in Purva Phalguni shows a past life where the soul enjoyed the fruits of its karma, but Ketu will always be uncomfortable with the good life. As a result the psyche harbours feelings of guilt regarding pleasure and fun. In fact the enjoyments of the past life were a break in the journey of the soul. Now the circumstances of life are tougher. Rahu in its own nakshatra in Saturn's sign of Aquarius, forces the ego to be given up and pleasures and desires discarded for a life of asceticism and purity. This is difficult for Rahu as it has forgotten its spiritual roots and fights against the spiritualising process. However as it learns to give up its individuality and material attachments a new light shines, leading to another level of development. The relationship between the two nakshatra rulers is an excellent one as Venus and Rahu are friends. So despite the difficulties that Ketu creates for Rahu, this axis can connect easily.

Rahu in Purva Bhadra (20°00Aquarius to 3°20 Pisces)
Ketu in Purva Phalguni (20°00 to 26°40 Leo) or
Uttara Phalguni (26°40 Leo to 3°20 Virgo)
Rahu in Purva Bhadra will have Ketu placed in either Purva Phalguni or Uttara Phalguni. Purva Bhadra gives the soul courage to change the course of its life. Purva means first and Bhadra beautiful and this is where the soul first becomes aware of its true beauty. This is not physical beauty, but the beauty that shines through a person as a direct result of inner perfection. Rahu has to learn to exist without personal rewards and live a life for others in order to undertake this new soul journey. Jupiter, the ruler of Purva Bhadra, will help guide the demonic Rahu energy to a more spiritual one. Rahu in Purva Bhadra in Aquarius, struggles with crystalising karma from the restrictions imposed by past life crises and mental blockages. Whereas in Purva Bhadra in Pisces struggles with lessons of the mind and the acceptance of the divine path becomes easier. The ruling deity of Purva Bhadra is Aja Ekapada - the one footed goat. A goat may not be a particularly attractive animal, but it reveals its beauty by giving and supporting life. So it is for those with Rahu in Purva Bhadra. They may not consider themselves beautiful, they may not feel their karma is up to standard or their past actions those to be proud of, yet like the goat Aja, they can reveal their beauty by their actions. The giving of oneself to others unconditionally brings

about real transformation in the Rahu energy, as people start to look at beauty beyond the physical attributes.

The conflict between Purva Bhadra and Purva Phalguni

Purva Phalguni has the ability to accept the rewards of past life struggles but Ketu will feel uncomfortable with this good fortune. The soul will struggle to accept the solar beneficence of this nakshatra. There were many auspicious events and happiness of the material kind yet Ketu's nature could never be happy with that, so it would have initiated a search for a deeper meaning.

Rahu in Purva Bhadra and Ketu in Purva Phalguni appear to be in conflict over their chosen path. Ketu, the moksha karaka, has to experience the pleasures of material life and Rahu, the materialistic planet, has to experience spirituality. Yet this axis is working towards enlightenment. Ketu in Purva Phalguni shows a past life where materialism was enjoyed so the soul is now ready for the next level of development, which is shown through Rahu. Rahu in Purva Bhadra may fight with its spiritual role, but of all the planets Rahu has the greatest spiritual lessons to teach an individual. It forces the giving up of material ambitions and allows a change of destiny while still living within the material world.

The conflict between Purva Bhadra (Aq) and Uttara Phalguni (Leo)

The light dawns that there is more to life than purely earthly attachment, and in Uttara Phalguni Ketu considers the notion of finding enlightenment. Ketu colours the mind of the individual towards doing good for others. Rahu in Purva Bhadra tries to fulfil its desires through service to others, but its initial reaction is to take all the glory for itself. This part of Purva Bhadra is in Aquarius and its ruler Saturn has no place for larger-than-life egos. So Rahu has to face reality. Jupiter as the ruler of Purva Bhadra will also guide Rahu towards its right path. Meanwhile Ketu is in the Leo part of Uttara Phalguni, a nakshatra that is also ruled by the Sun, so the relationship is of the eclipser and the eclipsed. This karmic relationship sees one darkening the light of the other yet revealing its beauty in another way. The spiritual path of Ketu is obstructed in Leo Uttara Phalguni but the eclipse itself reveals another reality. This can be confusing because Rahu receives no guidance towards its new path, leaving the individual to struggle to itself. It is important to recognise your false ego and your past life blocks.

The conflict between Purva Bhadra (Pisces) and Uttara Phalguni (Virgo)

In Purva Bhadra Rahu moves into idealistic Pisces. Purva Bhadra deals with expansion of the mind where the need is to trust and merge into a oneness with the ultimate – it is near the end of one cycle of the soul's journey. The symbol of Purva Bhadra is the sword and it is the sword that relentlessly cuts away at the past in order to fashion a new tomorrow. Ketu is now placed in Uttara Phalguni which is in Virgo, so has to learn discipline in preparation for the spiritual task ahead. The past life may have been full of service and duty as Ketu tried to atone for its actions, and this guilt is now passed to Rahu. It must recognise that the restrictions of the past life are no longer there and the opportunity is being given to take the final steps towards self realisation.

Rahu in Uttara Bhadra (3°20 to 16°40 Pisces) and Ketu in Uttara Phalguni (3°20 to 10°00 Virgo) or Hasta (10°00 to 16°40 Virgo)

Rahu in Uttara Bhadra will have Ketu placed in either Uttara Phalguni or Hasta. Rahu is in Pisces ruled by Jupiter but in a nakshatra ruled by restrictive Saturn. Jupiter eventually gives the wisdom to face all this adversity in search of its spiritual roots and Pisces symbolises the end of the spiritual journey. Uttara Bhadra indicates a journey to a beautiful place yet the steps Rahu takes to reach this place will initially be wrong. It is at a threshold of change that cannot be expressed through self-will or personal importance, and life experiences will lead it to give up this ego. As we go into the last stages of the nodal experience the issues become more intense, and the pain an individual feels from these experiences is more acute. Once you can merge with the dark night sky where everything becomes one creativity will unfold and the day will start anew. Rahu in Uttara Bhadra shows the pressure on the soul to let go of its fears and move into the final journey towards maturity

The conflict between Uttara Bhadra and Uttara Phalguni

In a past life Ketu in Uttara Phalguni began directing the soul towards its higher journey while living life on earth. These people were aware of their good fortune but it frustrated them to know that this destiny was tying them to the earthly domain. Uttara Phalguni stands for directed activity, so we must look towards making plans and not give in to momentary influences and thoughtless actions. As this axis brings the spiritual journey to a close there may be many crises face. There are no easy choices from the past life – the journey that could not be completed – and now Rahu has the burden of finishing this. The rulerships of the Sun and Saturn are significant as they represent both life and death. The Sun, reflecting the soul, begins its journey to find lost components in a past life and needs to pay a karmic debt whenever it embarks on a journey to the earth. Saturn's restrictions now stand in Rahu's way as the final karmic debts need to be paid. This is an unsettling axis since there is no going back, yet the future is uncertain. Rahu Ketu's house position (especially Ketu) will shed light on the specific past life issues to be resolved before Rahu can be free to take its final steps.

The conflict between Uttara Bhadra and Hasta

Hasta, ruled by the Moon, is placed entirely in the sign of Virgo ruled by Mercury. The intuitiveness of the Moon allows you to look beyond the ties of the material world but it was the intellectual part of Hasta that restricted the spiritual growth. Ketu in Hasta brings a lot of frustrations into this life but the essence of this placement is the ability to recognise life beyond its present restrictions. This axis deals with the conflicts of the mind and its illusions. Saturn rules Rahu and the Moon rules Ketu so the inheritance is emotional. As Saturn and Moon have a difficult relationship, emotions of the past become one of the burdens that Rahu has to offload. The perceived need for tranquillity and emotional happiness is so great that Rahu in Uttara Bhadra feels that it must actively seeks happiness. Saturn as its ruler will teach some pretty harsh lessons but that is the illusion. Taking stock and allowing the soul to develop towards a more spiritual state will create more happiness.

Rahu in Revati (16°40 to 30°00 Pisces) and Ketu in Hasta (16°40 to 23°20 Virgo) or Chitra (23°20 to 30°00 Virgo)

Revati is the final nakshatra for Rahu and enlightenment is possible from here. Enlightenment is understanding the purpose of life, being content with this particular moment of the journey. When we cease questioning life and accept its restrictions it opens another level of consciousness to us. Rahu in Revati is ruled by Mercury, the planet that brings the material and spiritual worlds together, and Rahu and Mercury are friends. As Revati's ruling deity is Pushan, a solar god who rules the death and rebirth of the Sun, this represents a time of utter stillness that carries the promise of light and new beginning. Rahu is now poised at this moment. It is in Revati that you sow the seeds for a future date. Revati means abundant or wealthy and Rahu in Revati tries to search for spiritual wealth in this life time and finds it no easy task. The final piece of the cycle of the soul's journey is about to be revealed and you must be ready to accept the move into that space of darkness and stillness. The acceptance of life as it is now allows you to take the final plunge into the next cycle of incarnation. Rahu is essentially unfulfilled unless it finds its spiritual essence and here it gets the opportunity to taste amrita. Through the practice of meditation, sacrifice and spiritual discipline amrita completes Rahu's journey.

The conflict between Revati and Hasta

Hasta wants an individual to change and grow in different directions. The inner urge is to stride ahead but external forces restrict it. Souls are guided to a life of renunciation and public service in the community, but are also a force for renewal. Ketu in Hasta is happy with the path of renunciation yet this was expressed before within material constraints. The Moon's rulership now brings movement and changing perspectives. This Revati Hasta axis is important as the soul has experienced one cycle of soul growth and is about to embark on the next. Ketu in Hasta worked towards a voluntary renunciation that created an emptiness within as it was unable to enjoy past life pleasures. Its rejection also lost its ability to be in touch with its emotions. Now Rahu has the responsibility to fulfil this life path. But for Rahu to experience happiness, it has to stop seeking it from outside and remember that it truly lies within. Rahu has matured to a great degree, but before the next steps can be taken the fear of failure has to be lost and the intuition trusted.

The conflict between Revati and Chitra

Chitra reflects the potential of the soul and the Chitra individual has two types of life experience: one in which it is almost unaware of its spiritual potential and the other where situations force it to recognise its higher nature. The personality is reformed but the process is painful as the ego has to be cut away so that the inner soul can emerge. Chitra is ruled by Mars and Ketu acts like Mars, so both are spiritual warriors with courage to face adversity. Chitra is tamasic in nature and Revati is sattvic. The past life was immersed in material darkness but now it has the opportunity to become pure and sacred. The story of Vasuki, the demon who transformed himself into a pure person, is prominent here. Rahu had the ability to taste the amrita once and will always aspire towards it again. Now Rahu has to change its way of thinking and allow the darkness to fade away. Part of the Rahu Ketu cycle is to expose our human failings then give us opportunities to rise above them. The essence of this whole struggle is encapsulated in Revati Chitra. Ketu indicates the past life in the world of darkness, yet some experiences showed the true reflection of its soul. Now Rahu looks for this wealth, and the answers are within.

7

KARMIC EXPERIENCES - NODAL CONJUNCTIONS

Planets in the same houses as the karmic axis indicate the past life connections we bring into this life. Some of these issues still have to be worked out, but others will take us to new heights if we focus on them with perseverance. Planets develop unusual traits when they are with Rahu or Ketu: Rahu usually enhances the basic quality of the planet forcing us to experience its issues to the fullest extent - it magnifies the experience for better or worse - while Ketu overshadows the planets and pinpoints karma we need to release from previous lives. Ketu's conjunction with planets can also cause a pattern of continual rejection to develop. This can however be broken with a deeper analysis of the inner self and an understanding of the connection to a past life.

In vedic astrology any planets conjunct Rahu or Ketu are described as 'eclipsed'. This is not a physical phenomenon but a metaphorical description of what Rahu and Ketu do to the planets involved, releasing psychic energy and causing inner turmoil. Often the planet behaves contrary to what would generally be expected. Naturally, because Rahu and Ketu are the opposite ends of an axis, any conjunction to Rahu also means an opposition to Ketu.

Planets in the Mouth of the Serpent

Rahu Ketu are represented as serpents. The image of a planet being in the mouth of the serpent graphically describes how Rahu or Ketu will be experienced more intensely during the period that they are applying or moving towards a conjunction with another planet. The planet concerned feels the presence of the nodes like a large shadow looming over it. As Rahu and Ketu always transit in retrograde motion, the planet at a lesser degree than themselves is going to feel their impact acutely. For example, if Rahu or Ketu is placed at 10 degrees

Aries and your Moon is placed at 9 degrees Aries, your Moon will be in the mouth of the serpent and your experience of Rahu or Ketu will be extremely powerful. If the Moon in this example were placed at 12 degrees of Aries, it has moved to the other side of Rahu Ketu's retrograde motion and the influence of the nodes would be less intense. There are no exact number of degrees given in the classical texts to qualify a planet being in the mouth of the serpent, but in my opinion the planets should be within five degrees of the nodes.

The Sun and Moon

The Sun and the Moon suffer the most from conjunctions to Rahu or Ketu. In the myth of Naga Vasuki, the Sun and Moon were his enemies and the ability of the nodes to eclipse the light of the Sun and Moon makes a conjunction with either of them very difficult.

Analysing the Conjunctions

We need to remember three factors when considering the impact of Rahu Ketu:

1.   Their own energies
2.   Their rulerships of signs and houses
3.   Their *karaka* energies. Karaka means signification: the Moon signifies the mother; the Sun, the father; Mars, courage and brothers; Mercury, intellect; Jupiter, teacher, husbands (in the case of women), and sons; Venus, marriage or the wife in male charts; Saturn, work or discipline.

For example, when Ketu is conjunct Venus it shows a past life connection to all Venusian energies and a present dilemma over those issues. As Venus rules Taurus and Libra, the impact of Ketu will also be felt on those two signs. For example if you had Taurus rising, then Venus would also become your *lagna* lord (Ascendant ruler) and your life would be coloured by Ketu and the influence of the past. If you had Scorpio rising, then Venus would rule your 7th house of relationships and 12th house of loss. In addition to the above you would study the karakas of Venus, which is the karaka of relationships for everyone male or female, but also refers to the wife in male charts. A Venus/Ketu conjunction will have an impact on these relationships regardless of its house rulerships.

Patterns of Past Life - Ketu Conjunctions

As Ketu represents past lives it focuses particularly on the things you did wrong or had not worked on sufficiently and which now form a part of your karma in this life. It is usually the negative issues we remember most, as the positive aspects of life we take for granted. Ketu is the sting in the Rahu Ketu tail: it takes away what it gives you, often in cycles of seven years, and is generally thought to come of age at 48. Up until that time you are likely to experience its negative side, but as you grow older Ketu starts taking less and giving more.

In your horoscope for this lifetime, Ketu indicates areas or people in your past lives where or with whom you have unfinished business. Ketu has a tendency to remember all experiences, absorbing everything and leaving a feeling of guilt that is difficult to relinquish. When planets are conjunct the Ketu part of the axis, it alerts you to a vulnerability over issues which have to be worked out on an inner level. These issues cannot be resolved by new experiences but by understanding old ones and letting them go. Many difficult aspects of life need to be accepted especially if they are created by Ketu conjunctions. The aim of Ketu is renunciation. Conjunct any planet, it will encourage you to give up something to do with that planet's energies.

Ketu and the Sun

The Sun is the soul, your future karma and direction in life. Ketu conjunct the Sun indicates a powerful past life karma which is obstructing your growth in the present, blocking the light from your future unless you deal with its adverse issues. The restrictions usually work on the mental plane and at times it is difficult to recognise the problems without deep reflection. Learn to let go of past problems and create new karma in their place.

Ketu conjunct the Sun can also appear in the material world as a loss of reputation. You may receive no help from official organisations when you need it, or you may reject authority and work with the democratic principle. The Sun/Ketu combination is often seen in the charts of people who protest against governments and large corporations. Their protest is not always about issues but about the power of these governments and multi-national companies.

It shows itself most often in a difficult relationship with your father. This is one of the most challenging conjunctions of the horoscope, as your entire identity rests with the Sun. Past life issues with fathers are brought over into the present, and this conjunction implies that you are dealing with some form of rejection or perceived non-appreciation from your father. The distance between yourself and your father also creates an identity crisis within yourself. Past life issues involving parents show deep-rooted problems that need to be worked out so try to forgive your father and yourself. Indian philosophy believes we choose our parents to experience and pay karmic debts.

A Sun Ketu conjunction has to learn to live life differently. The darkening or eclipse of the Sun suggests that strong psychic energy is part of this conjunction and that a re-birth or extreme transformation is experienced as part of this incarnation. As you struggle to leave behind the darkness and the traditional paternal role models, feelings of rejection and guilt are relinquished and you find a new self-identity.

Ketu and the Moon

The Moon represents the mind, and Ketu is the keeper of past life knowledge as well as being *moksha karaka*, the significator for spiritual salvation. Their conjunction is not an easy combination. Ketu conjunct the Moon gives great psychic powers and the ability to hear voices from the past, but this gift can get out of control and lead to emotional imbalances if not properly harnessed. The psychic powers of Ketu and the Moon can confuse the mind with past-life knowledge causing irrational fear, and in extreme cases suicidal tendencies. It is important for those with this combination to concentrate on their inner development. Yoga, spiritual discipline, meditation and sattvik (pure) living can be used as important shields in protecting the mind from unabridged information from the past. When you are able to control or harness this energy, you can use the Ketu/Moon conjunction more positively.

Many events in this life will have their roots in powerful past life connections, particularly concerning the mother. Problems with mothers in past lives must now be addressed in the relationship with your mother in this one - it is considered a gift from past life karmas and this conjunction shows major issues with maternal love. Your mother may be unusual or different from others or there may be a sense of rejection between you. Your mother may have a control over your life, which is very frustrating. Whatever the situation, you carry the guilt of your feelings with you forever. The Ketu Moon suggests that you need to examine the complexities of this maternal relationship, so that the negative feelings don't colour your relationships with other people. Stop the pattern of blame and rejection. Understanding, forgiveness and acceptance are important tools in healing this challenging relationship.

There is a struggle between the Moon's search for happiness and Ketu's ideal of renunciation and you may bring into this life a certain feeling of unhappiness from previous lives for which there appears to be no apparent cure. The crisis can only be resolved by clearly identifying the past life issues and compartmentalising them. Ketu desires moksha - a situation few can achieve. Its extreme idealism sets very high targets for happiness so the Ketu Moon feels it can only be happy under impossible conditions. The solution to this is to identify with the simple pleasures of life: the beauty of a sunset, the smell of a first spring rainfall. The past you cannot change, the future is yet to be experienced, so try to find the pleasure in today. When past life actions cease to cause pain and there is no anxiety about the future, you will start finding peace and happiness within.

Ketu and Mars

A Ketu Mars conjunction indicates that you bring issues concerning anger, violence, courage and the experiencing of new beginnings from past lives. You may fear violence or have some past life experience connected to war and bloodshed which is still carried in your subconscious. Ketu and Mars are similar energies, both prone on a negative level to rage and a destructive tendency to cause accident and injury. On a positive level they aim for the highest, and have the courage to reach pure and noble objectives despite the obstacles faced. Try to calm down - control your impulsive tendencies and turn them into leadership qualities.

One of the real issues of the Ketu Mars conjunction is the inability to understand and be happy with your own power. This is especially true of women. People with this combination may try to ignore their own strength and reject their capacity to lead. In many cases they will try to express this through others, yet deep within themselves they are extremely powerful. This can create frustration and power struggles as others are probably not willing to live out these needs. If you have this placement, I feel you need to be honest with yourself and understand your own strength and power. Mars Ketu is a good combination for technical studies and mathematics. Many engineers and computer scientists are born with this conjunction, as are good leaders in the police and armed forces.

The Ketu Mars conjunction also indicates that you have a special connection with your brothers in this life. If you do not have a brother you may feel the lack of this relationship strongly and substitute platonic male relationships to fill the absent need.

Ketu and Mercury

Ketu is the keeper of the Book of Life Knowledge, which also represents the knowledge of astrology, the vedas and tantra; Mercury is the intellectual mind. Although Ketu with Mercury may inhibit your ability to use your mind well, this is a very good situation for abstract thinkers. Here the intellect has access to the knowledge contained within Ketu. You can be intuitive, psychic and clairvoyant. You may have great interest in knowledge from the past: astrology, history, archaeology and the study of the inner secrets of mind like psychology. You may not have used your intellectual energies properly in a past life, but now you need to use your knowledge for the benefit of others - perhaps through teaching or writing. Ketu also gives the ability to block your mind from painful episodes. This obviously has its advantages but unless you are actively connected with using your mind, you may feel unfulfilled and unhappy.

People with the Mercury Ketu combination can be very intelligent but often do not recognise their own qualities. A brilliant student may give up an academic career to work in a position where the intellect is not fully exercised. If Mercury ruled the 7th and 10th house for Sagittarius rising, a person may give up both a career and a relationship to voluntarily follow an idealistic life of poverty in a search for perfection. Mercury Ketu gives a sharp mind but with very non-traditional qualities.

Mercury has the ability for duplicity and the combination with Ketu can cause the intellect to become devious and underhand. This highlights the poisonous aspect of Ketu and the past life. It is your choice how you are going to use your intellect. Here you need to be aware of how karma initiated now can effect you at a later stage and you should try to use your mind for the good of others.

Mercury is the significator of childhood, of sisters and stepfamilies, so a Ketu conjunction shows that karma has to be worked out with these issues. It might mean a life without a sister or a rejecting of sisterly love. Your childhood can be unusual and eccentric. You may learn to deal with stepfamilies, either having step brothers and sisters when you are young or step-children through your marriage later. (This will be indicated by the houses that Mercury rules or the positioning of the axis. The 6th house deals particularly with stepfamilies).

Ketu and Jupiter

Jupiter conjunct the karmic axis shows that relationships, children and knowledge were and are the big issues in life. This conjunction in a woman's chart, where Jupiter represents her partner, might manifest in her choice of a partner who is not socially acceptable. She may become involved with men who are working out powerful karma in their own life, perhaps with problems through drugs, alcohol, or relationship baggage. Even showing itself more positively, a woman with Ketu and Jupiter together is not likely to marry someone run-of-the-mill! She may experiment with a non-traditional relationship or be involved with someone who is not from her own background. There may be unfinished business brought into this life from the past concerning partners and it is necessary to understand the relationship on a much deeper level than the purely physical. You are likely to be extremely sensitive to rejection, even if your partner is not rejecting you, and it is important to discuss these feelings together before it becomes a major issue. Ketu and Jupiter can also indicate a karmic relationship with your sons, especially your eldest son. You may experience separation, extreme attachment or guilt in this connection.

Past life connections draw you to certain types of philosophy and you may experiment with different religions or faiths until you find the right one. This may possibly be a doctrine you were unable to follow in a past life. Gurus or teachers are likely to enter your life from completely unexpected directions, and you will be willing to learn from many different teachers - probably from foreign countries. This combination gives rise to a Guru Chandala Yoga which underlines your interest in foreign philosophies to the extent that you may reject your own culture and its thinking. Such issues were considered very negative at the time the Vedas were written, but in today's multi-cultural society there is no stigma attached to interest or involvement in a culture or religion other than your own.

Ketu and Venus

The Ketu Venus combination brings an unresolved past life relationship into the context of the current life. Unless you understand the subtle realities of the relationship pattern, you may find your experiences painful or unhappy. You could attract partners who carry lots of emotional or spiritual baggage. Ketu Venus often makes you experience the issue of rejection very acutely. This can lead to multiple relationships that do not bring lasting happiness as, fearing rejection, you tend to discard them before they have a chance to develop.

As with Ketu and Jupiter in a woman's chart, a man with Ketu and Venus may choose a partner who is not acceptable to his caste or class, or to his family. One of my clients with this combination was helping his lover overcome the addiction she had brought into the relationship. This combination brings added problems to a partnership, so be prepared to deal with it.

More generally, Ketu and Venus indicate a relationship that is unusual or unorthodox in some way. You may reject the institution of marriage, or relate to each other only on a spiritual level. You might experiment with sexuality through gay or lesbian relationships. A Venus Ketu marriage can also been seen as a protest against society and its restrictions. Venus is the significator of marriage in all charts, but with Ketu this creates problems because it may injure the marriage through its need to wander or renounce. Ketu Venus conjunctions have to be handled with great sensitivity. You know you will have to deal with issues surrounding your relationships, so you can choose to work with them or ignore them. The important lesson that comes from Ketu Venus is to stop rejecting. Moving from one relationship to another will not fulfil your expectation of perfection as no one person can meet these requirements. You must look at the positive areas of your present relationship and be willing to discuss any difficulties. It is only in extreme cases that harmony is beyond reach. Mostly Ketu brings many different colours into your relationships, and by connecting to them you can enjoy great spiritual happiness.

Ketu and Saturn

Ketu and Saturn show specific past life issues, which crystallize now. The houses of the karmic axis will show areas in which you are likely to have difficult experiences in this life, but of course they do not have to be insurmountable. Faced with problems, you develop an ability to grow and deal with them, and this actually gives you immense strength.

As Ketu acts like Mars, Ketu and Saturn are seen as the greatest enemies in the zodiac. Although they share the same purpose of guiding you towards your true spiritual path, they act in very different ways. Saturn separates and Ketu renounces. Saturn operates in the here and now - in the real world - and Ketu operates on the inner plane. Ketu is the carrier of past knowledge and Saturn forces past karmic issues to be faced in practical life. Saturn keeps you firmly anchored in the material world and insists that you confront issues in this lifetime, but Ketu wants you to renounce the material world and move on. This placement can encourage travel and living abroad with no need for a firm home base. Saturn and Ketu are wanderers in different ways making this a tough combination to have. You are forced to let go of attachments while still trying to face up to life. Ketu is a mendicant and is happy to live in poverty, never understanding Saturn's need for discipline and hard work. This can appear as rejection of the rat race and a protest against discipline and hard work. The mind wants to avoid Saturn's obstructions but having to face them becomes the greatest life lesson. It signifies a major crisis issue that can change the focus of your life.

Magnifying the Present - Rahu Conjunctions

Rahu's aim is to experience life to the fullest possible extent, and its conjunction with a planet encourages those qualities to the extreme. No planet remains unscathed from its association.

Rahu wants life on a large scale: it can be like an experience with drugs where the desire for enhanced senses leads to the loss of both control and reality. Rahu encourages an individual to go for overblown high fidelity experiences with no boundaries, and its conjunction with a planet can make these experiences surreal. But the pattern of the Rahu fixes must be broken. It is vital to learn control and discipline for it is the lack of control that brings the fear or paranoia associated with Rahu.

Rahu conjunctions always indicate that your competition is with your own demons and not with the world. The planet it conjuncts becomes the conduit through which Rahu expresses its shadows and struggles. Once you understand this, you will be able to confront your fears with greater equilibrium. Rahu can create a fear of experiencing what the planet represents. For example,

Rahu conjunct the Sun may indicate that you fear your father or have some difficulty with authority: there may be a great competitiveness with your father, driving you to be more successful than him or trying to live up to his unrealistic expectations. 'Unrealistic' is the key word, because Rahu always represents this.

Rahu and the Sun

Any connection between Rahu and the Sun is considered an eclipse. This is usually a difficult combination because Rahu creates problems with the connection to your eternal soul. But it is an identity crisis that is different from the Ketu Sun conjunction as in this situation you want to expand your identity outwardly and become a powerful, successful person. You can make an immense mark on worldly issues and in this way Rahu enhances the qualities of the Sun. Your life has a clear direction and success is indicated: a high social position, fame and achievement. However, as Rahu behaves like Saturn, who is not the best of friends with the Sun, the negative side is also enhanced: over-ambition, selfishness and a rigidity of ideas. There may also be a fear of failure, as the type of success and power you visualise is not necessary realistic or available to everyone. Forever expanding your horizons and adding to your ambitions, you may go for that one ambition too much and create failure. In fact the Rahu Sun conjunction suggests the block to your ultimate success is yourself. There may be strong overseas connections and foreigners can sometimes harm your reputation, or you may be involved in scandal. If you learn to control your ambitions and be happy with your present success, your light will shine more naturally.

Rahu and the Moon

The Moon is afraid of Rahu. Rahu represents darkness and its mission is to detach you from the pleasures of life. When the Moon is placed with Rahu all the things which the Moon represents will suffer. Rahu causes fear, anxiety and distrust. Issues from the past may impede your growth in the form of fears or phobias that you cannot rationalise and you may lean too heavily on drink or drugs. Your relationship with your mother is eclipsed in some way (perhaps you were separated from her when very young) and there are hidden factors in your relationships with women in general.

The Rahu Moon combination instils a fear within, that inclines you to see your world in shadows. This is the most difficult combination for the Moon to have, as it relates to emotional happiness and Rahu leads you down the wrong paths in search of it. The need for happiness is so great that you try to experience it in extreme form and then become unrealistic about how to get it, and even begin to fear it. Rahu has the ability to make you see things negatively and it is important not to put yourself in situations where your mental equilibrium is disturbed. Through meditation, chanting, spirituality, yoga and pure diet you can help yourself come to terms with Rahu. Trying to look for the positive in life and within yourself will also help to allay your fears. I think the most important factor to examine is expectations you have of yourself. Are you being realistic? Many of our fears are the result of an inability to fulfil our desires. If we give up the desires, learn to be honest and face up to our fears, we have a better chance of finding that elusive happiness.

You will remember that in the myth of Naga Vasuki the ocean was churned up: with Rahu and the Moon together your emotions are likely to be in a similar state. However, in the myth the nectar of immortality was discovered, so the consequences of having Rahu conjunct the Moon need not be all negative. People with this combination should practice yoga and mantras to help overcome the influence of Rahu and the fear of moving towards the future. The house placement is very important with this conjunction. For example it will be much harder to deal with in the 8th house than in the 9th.

Rahu and Mars

Rahu acts like Saturn, which is not friendly with Mars, so this is a tense, difficult conjunction. You are always testing your power and courage. It could show outward courage and inner fear. Mars does not like limitation so when it is placed within the karmic axis it will try to externalise all its previous powers and may not be able to control its potential. The power unleashed can be destructive so it is better kept in check.

Rahu highlights athletic prowess and Martian sexual energy. Passion, courage and an adventurous spirit are emphasised and this is a good combination for an achievement-orientated career, but beware of an impetuous temper and an inclination towards violence. Rahu and Mars can also be accident-prone. Rahu has a political mind and Mars is about leadership and power, so the combination can produce a formidable politician who does not accept defeat easily and uses every means at their disposal - fair or foul - to achieve success. The Rahu Mars combination always results in some kind of power either at home or at work. The need to dominate is so strong that it is essential to recognise this as a negative quality within oneself. Mars and Rahu has many positive ways of channeling its energies and can achieve the impossible through courage and power. The Rahu Mars courage can be a great boost if you choose to follow a spiritual path. Mahatma Gandhi, the great freedom fighter for Indian independence, had this conjunction and used its powers positively. Mars and Rahu placed in the 10th or 6th house can become very powerful.

Rahu and Mercury

This can be a good combination as Rahu and Mercury are friends. Mercury represents pure intellect and Rahu magnifies this to its greatest extend. Together they can give a powerful intelligence, a sharp mind, good powers of communication and knowledge of the hidden side of life. Past life intellect now has a channel to express itself in the strongest possible way. However Vasuki was a demon using powers for his own gain, and both he and Mercury are ambivalent energies. You may be intelligent, flexible and charming but perhaps not especially honest! You might use your powers of mind to promote yourself rather than for the greater good. Of course, in today's world that may seem quite acceptable but it may not help you on the path to true enlightenment.

Rahu Mercury can also create phobias and mental imbalances. Intellectual blocks, fear of failure, inability to express oneself clearly and sudden ups and downs in your mind are all due to Rahu. You may try to impress others intellectually, believing that you need to scale another height of mental dominance to prove yourself superior. A poor self-image is your fear. Others do not see the struggle for dominance, already thinking you are intellectually admirable, yet this is not what you feel. This conjunction can create depression and lack of confidence unless you understand that the problem lies within yourself. The fears highlighted are of your own creation and the competition is with yourself, not others.

Rahu and Jupiter

Jupiter's connection with the karmic axis suggests that you experience expansiveness and beneficence - the conjunction enhances good luck. Jupiter creates a balance between Rahu and Ketu, teaching them wisdom, knowledge of ritual and higher philosophy. As Rahu represents where we are heading in life, its combination with Jupiter indicates you are seeking the very highest knowledge and learning. Jupiter enhances the karmic axis making karmic issues easier to understand. Rahu also represents foreigners, so you could be drawn to foreign philosophies and religions, but the connection of Rahu to Jupiter can spoil the energy of Jupiter in its purist form and while on the material level there can be an abundance of financial gains, you need to be careful not to overdo things. Rahu and Jupiter together do not necessarily give happiness, just wealth.

In a woman's chart, Jupiter represents her partner and Rahu is the significator of foreigners, so a woman with Rahu Jupiter may be attracted to foreign men. She may also be attracted to men with hidden qualities, perhaps devious ones, or she might never know what her husband is up to! One way or another Jupiter will not give her a traditional marriage partner. As Rahu represents fear, it may create a fear of losing your partner and a danger of becoming suspicious and possessive. Rahu enjoys experiencing relationships with great intensity and in extreme cases you may be confronted with the problem of multiple relationships. This is likely to bring a sense of dissatisfaction rather than fulfilment. Jupiter also represents the eldest son. It might mean that your eldest son is somehow 'foreign' to you. The conjunction is often associated with adoption.

Jupiter Rahu creates a yoga known as Guru Chandala yoga which theoretically means that your ideas and philosophies have been spoiled. However the word 'spoilt' here can mean following a foreign philosophy, which does not create the same problems today as it did in earlier times; if you were living within a rigid religious environment, it would obviously bring difficulties. Also beware of meeting corrupt gurus or teachers who are not on the correct path. (For more information see the chapter on The Yogas.)

Rahu and Venus

Venus and Rahu are friends, so this combination can give financial and material wealth. Rahu emphasises the charm and beauty of Venus but it can take away its purity. As Rahu does not recognise caste or class, a Rahu Venus conjunction enables you to move freely in any society. Rahu and Venus create a classless society for you.

Venus represents marriage generally, and in a man's chart specifically the kind of woman he will marry. A man may be attracted to foreign women or women who are not of his caste or class, or somone who has had a rich and varied past.

As with Rahu Jupiter, Rahu Venus can make you fearful of losing your relationship and this can make you possessive and suspicious. Also Rahu's need to experience relationship may take you down the road to multiple unions. This could potentially lead to a deep sense of failure so it is important to break the pattern. I think the greatest problem of the Rahu Venus conjunction is the lack of trust it generates within you. You need to work on this element in yourself.

Rahu and Saturn

As Rahu already acts like Saturn, in conjunction they can be doubly malefic. The difficulty is the level at which they operate: Saturn acts physically, Rahu psychologically. But Rahu is an achiever and Saturn an ascetic, so with this combination there is a double dose of wisdom through limitation and separation. Their purpose is to encourage detachment from this world. If you are patient and able to acknowledge the positive energy of Saturn as the teacher of ultimate truths and the guide of your spiritual direction, Rahu and Saturn will give you immense patience to understand the karma of life and cosmic law represented by the nodes. You will learn to recognise your limitations and your part in Rahu Ketu's learning process. It is a difficult position and needs great maturity of the soul to understand it.

The Rahu Saturn combination is good for a political career as Saturn stands for the democratic principle and Rahu for politics. This is a special talent as it can allow you to work with democratic or labour relations on a large or international scale.

8

THE PLANETS AND THE NODAL NAKSHATRA

Rahu Ketu rule three nakshatras each and their influence can be felt if planets are placed within these nakshatras. The Moon's position is the most important as it shows the beginning of your dasha cycle, but other planets are also influenced by their placement in Rahu or Ketu nakshatras as their change of character stimulates the karmic influences into your life.

Rahu Nakshatras

Rahu rules   Ardra (6° 40' - 20° 00' Gemini)

Swati (6°40' - 20°00' Libra)

Shatabishak (6°40' - 20°00' Aquarius)

These are all in the air triplicity. Mercury (intellectual ability), Venus (pleasure) and Saturn (righteous behaviour) will all have their qualities enhanced as a result of their association with Rahu.

Ardra   symbol - precious stone or a human head

deity - Rudra

Ardra means green, moist. It is situated entirely in Gemini, which is ruled by Mercury. Rahu rules Ardra in its entirety, which explains the main focus for the nakshatra. In the myth Rahu (as Vasuki) drank the nectar which made him immortal, and therefore as the ruler of Ardra he also has great ambitions. Mercury indicates that the sphere of activity is going to be intellectual so Rahu's search here is for intellectual perfection.

    The symbol of the precious stone or jewel shows the ability to absorb the kinetic, mystical and spiritual energy from the Sun. Jewels are known to absorb energies and transmit them to the wearer, so Ardra has the capacity to absorb powers and then use them.

The other symbol of Ardra is the head. The brain is formed by experiences from the karma of the past and the mind can work both ways, either for good or ill. The symbolism of both the head and jewel stand for ideas, thinking and the mind.

The overall influence of Ardra represents the duality of Gemini: Rahu's lust for immortality, Mercury's dualistic mind and intellect. Both can be used to enhance the world or destroy it. At the cosmic stage of Ardra, there is a conflict on the outer level that makes us dissatisfied with our present surroundings and begin a search for answers. This can be through knowledge, communication or the occult.

Rudra, the God of Destruction, is Ardra's presiding deity, and Rudra is a form of Shiva. His mission is to destroy ignorance, so he directs our consciousness towards knowledge and finding the answers about this manifestation for ourselves. At Ardra we start to learn about the Law of Nature. For the first time we become dissatisfied with the nature of our lives and start expanding our horizons.

If the Sun is placed in Ardra it indicates a soul striving for achievement - both in a spiritual context and in the material world. The Moon in Ardra reflects emotional fears and instability, perhaps through difficulties with the mother. The first dasha will be that of Rahu so many of these issues will be dealt with at a very early stage. Mars in Ardra fights for intellectual superiority and this can be a good combination for writers. Mercury in Ardra is excellently placed giving great strength of mind and powerful intellect. It is good for both writers and astrologers. Jupiter in Ardra gives intellectual wisdom, but the position may create relationship problems for women. Venus in Ardra is inclined to be fickle and have many relationships, although it is excellent for media and communication success. Saturn in Ardra is noticeably strong and good for political ambitions.

Swati　　　　symbol - coral
　　　　　　　　deity - Vayu, the god of wind and life breath

Planets in Swati indicate the depth of the soul's involvement in materialism. The indicator of the soul in the chart, the Sun, is debilitated here. Under Swati, the impulse is about material gain. The Libran ruler Venus oversees the earthly needs in an individual, so combining this with Rahu it adds further to the desire for success in finance and wealth. Many millionaires are born with their Moon in Swati. The location of this nakshatra in Libra indicates that full involvement in earthy, materialistic pleasures brings dissatisfaction because the scales will be too heavy on one side. Libra is a stage of life when we start to think about spiritual meaning, but only once other urges have been fulfilled. The subjective spirit wants to expand but the material sheaths restrict. Equilibrium is reached by these opposing tendencies allowing the individual to maintain stability.

The symbol of Swati is coral, which has a hard outer shell but is self-propagating. It both affects and is affected by its marine environment, which can be an analogy of the human being who lives in a world which influences him yet is altered in turn by his impact on it.

The presiding deity of Swati is Vayu, who rules the material world along with Agni (fire) and Varuna (water). The area of operation is the atmosphere - the Prana - the life breath. Vayu controls the desires and the intellect making Swati essentially materialistic and involved in mundane pursuits.

The Sun is debilitated in Swati emphasising the attachment to the material world. It is a good position for lawyers and business, and partnership issues are always important. The Moon in Swati shows stress and nervous energy, and as the first dasha will be Rahu, there may be a difficult childhood. Mars is not happily placed here as the psychological impact of Swati creates fears and shadows that warrior Mars finds difficult to deal with. Mercury in Swati is an excellent position however, making the person charming and a great communicator and also good at business. Jupiter will not function well here because it is in its inimical sign and nakshatra. This can bring out the negative qualities of Jupiter such as pride and an inflated ego. Jupiter in Swati gives the wrong type of advice. Venus in Swati is very strong, being in its own sign. Venus and Rahu are friends and bring excellent results, although you may still need to watch out over relationship issues. Saturn is also strong in Swati, almost reaching its exaltation.

Shatabhishak   symbol - hundred flowers or 100 demons
                            deity - Varuna

Shatabishak is entirely in the sign of Aquarius, ruled by Saturn, so Rahu's rulership of this nakshatra makes a difficult combination. The double Saturnian influence is best handled by directing our activities towards others and service to humanity. Here both Rahu and Saturn are concerned with changing the purpose of our life to give us the final answers, and Rahu does this on an internal level while Saturn works on the external. Restrictions, obstacles and transformation are likely to be encountered as aspects of Shatabishak.

With its symbol of the thousand-petalled flowers, Shatabishak is where the kundalini blossoms when we reach the full awareness of our consciousness. This is the stage in life where the Sahasara (crown) chakra is activated and Rahu brings forth its full power as the teacher of cosmic law. When the Moon is in Shatabishak its materialistic tendencies are shed completely and we can move into the next phase of spiritual development.

The presiding deity, Varuna, bestows knowledge and wisdom on the person so that a ray of light shines through him. This ray of light illuminates our perception and explains the real purpose of our soul and why we are here. It guides the person under the direction of Varuna towards a new approach to life

The Sun in Shatabhishak is never comfortable as Rahu creates a very unstable environment for the solar energy. The Moon initially has a tough time in this nakshatra too. As the first dasha will be Rahu, the childhood is likely to be one of shadowy experiences that are difficult to handle. Mars is among enemies in Shatabhishak, but it has the ability to fight the possible fears and paranoia and eventually deal with them. It is not such a good position for Mercury as the planet is very close to its debilitation point and Rahu can create irrational behaviour and bring out unnecessary stresses and fears. Jupiter, which is at heart a traditionalist, will have to learn lessons of democracy and working for others in Shatabhishak as it works with the unconventional energies. Venus is extremely strong, but unorthodox. Saturn is also strong but will bring difficult lessons in Shatabhishak as it conquers the dark side of your nature to achieve greatness. Saturn will give you a tremendous ability to deal with pain and help to discipline yourself.

Ketu Nakshatras

Ketu rules		
	Ashwini	(0°00' - 13°20' Aries)
	Magha	(0°00' - 13°20' Leo)
	Mula	(0°00' - 13°20' Sagittarius)

All these are in the fire triplicity: they are the beginning stages in the cycles of life. Mars, the Sun and Jupiter, the rulers of Aries, Leo and Sagittarius, are friends with each other. Together they represent strength, the soul and wisdom, which will be heightened by Ketu; when the energy of these planets is well integrated we can reach towards moksha.

Ashwini
symbol - the head of a horse
deity - Ashwini Kumaras

Ashwini, the first nakshatra, is in the sign of Aries, which deals with birth, new life and the start of a new cycle. Ashwini indicates the beginning of the soul's journey in earthly life, and Ketu is the significator of moksha. Its rulership of the first nakshatra shows that the true reason for our manifestation on earth is to find spiritual liberation. This is the stage where the mind is still pure and we have not yet become entangled with the intricacies of life.

The Ashwins were twin sons of the Sun God. They were the celestial physicians with great healing powers. People born in Ashwini are great healers and have the ability to rejuvenate the old and give life to the dead. They can be successful on both the material and spiritual levels as Ashwini holds latent creative power.

The Sun, the significator of the soul and our inner consciousness, is exalted in Ashwini. This is an excellent position, bringing out its best qualities while staying pure and spiritual. Past life connections are very strong if the Moon is placed here, because Ketu is the planet that keeps the secrets of all past lives. As Ketu will be the first dasha to be experienced you may deal with issues of rejection during the early years of life. Mars in Ashwini preserves the purity of Martian action, and courage and the protection of humanity is powerfully indicated. Mercury is never happily placed in a Ketu nakshatra, so in Ashwini it feels blocked until it uses its intellect properly. The fiery quality can make Mercury impulsive and mentally aggressive. Jupiter will be strong with its wisdom connected to past life knowledge, but there can be a rejection of a more traditional way of life. Venus is not happy to be placed in a nakshatra of renunciation either and its position in Aswini can create relationship problems - but the inner quality of Venus will be influenced by spirituality. Saturn is weak here as it is moving towards its debilitation. Ketu forces the Saturnine energy to look back to a past life and forward to a new tomorrow. Saturn will not behave like its usual self in Aswini. There may be a rejection of the work ethic and democratic principles.

Magha   symbol - a house or a palanquin
                     deity - Pitris or the forefathers

Magha is the second nakshatra ruled by Ketu and Magha is in the sign of Leo ruled by the Sun. Magha means mighty, so people born in this nakshatra aspire towards greatness. The signs from Leo to Scorpio indicate the soul's full involvement in the pleasures and pains of earthly life, and Magha marks the beginning of this second cycle in the soul's journey. As Ketu, the significator of spiritual realisation, rules the starting point of this materialistic journey, it highlights the importance of experiencing the realities of life whilst still fulfilling the divine mission of the soul.

The symbols of Magha are a palanquin and a house. The house is an analogy of the human body, which is the tool used to carry out the spiritual mission. The palanquin is transport, an enclosed seat with a central rod made from a bamboo pole. The central rod represents the spinal cord and the knots in the pole are the chakra points. The people carrying the palanquin symbolise the organs of senses and action, which gives a clear direction to Magha that these must be conquered. The senses must become like servants, enabling the chakras to be activated in order to reach true understanding. At this stage however the direction is being given but not necessarily the answers.

Magha's ruling deity is the Pitris, who are the fathers of humanity with a mission to guide their children on the right course. The fathers only interfere in life if you are straying from the right path and Ketu and Pitris both guide the soul towards its special mission. Planets in Magha tend to be idealistic even if their purpose is only to fulfill materialistic needs. At times this creates misunderstandings causing others to suspect your honour and sincerity. Magha gives a lot materially, but the person ruled by Magha knows intuitively that material happiness is only an experience on the inner road to moksha.

The Sun, the significator of the soul and inner consciousness, is strong here in its own sign. The main star of Magha is the auspicious and royal Regulus, so there is promise of great success, and this Ketu nakshatra brings an idealistic approach. The Moon's placement is a difficult one however as Ketu will be the first dasha to be experienced. Issues of rejection are therefore likely during the very early years of life. Mars in Magha is strong both physically and mentally. Mercury is uncomfortable, yet this position gives Mercury a fiery intelligence and a fighting mind. Jupiter is not well placed in Magha as it is just out of its exaltation in Cancer and is never considered very strong. Ketu creates a barrier to Jupiter being able to express itself clearly. Venus in Magha is not strong either as it is spoiled by the Ketu energy. Neither is Saturn well placed because Magha deals with the individual greatness of human beings and Saturn believes in everyone's rights, so this positioning is immensely difficult for it. Your Saturn energy has to work in unorthodox ways and change its attitude if it is to be productive here.

Mula
symbol - the tail of a lion or an elephant's goad
deity - Nittriti

Mula is the third nakshatra ruled by Ketu and it heralds the final part of the soul's mission in its quest for enlightenment; this can be one of the most difficult nakshatras for planets to be situated in, especially the Moon.

An elephant's goad is used to guide the elephant in the correct direction. It represents the constant prodding or pain we experience in the search for our spiritual pathway. The lion uses his tail to express his anger or supremacy. These symbols show two opposite sides of the Mula characteristic. There can be immense anger directed at others as power is such a strong issue. Jupiter, as ruler of the sign, represents wisdom, and Ketu is the past karma we carry in the subconscious. If the latter is not being expressed or channelled properly it can lead to abuse of power.

The deity that rules Mula is Nittriti, the goddess of death and destruction.

It personifies the destruction of our material desires and creates the foundation for spiritual development. The pain experienced by the influence of Mula changes the personality as attachments to the lower nature and material tendencies have to be severed before the new spiritual beginning. This is the nakshatra of initiation towards spiritual realisation and Ketu fulfills its role as moksha karaka by pushing the soul towards its ultimate destination. Mula means root, also referring to the Muladhara chakra (the base chakra) where the kundalini power is activated.

In this nakshatra our basic psychology is subject to change and therefore Mula is a challenge for all planets situated here. However the Sun, the significator of the soul and inner consciousness, is finally able to reach towards its goal of self-realisation. It is the Moon that faces its greatest challenge, as Ketu will be the first dasha to be experienced and will throw up more karmic issues than any other. This dasha deals with the changing psychology of the mind, which is not an easy experience for a child - it is likely to have a great impact in later life. Mars is strong in Mula as it deals with adverse situations requiring courage and spiritual strength. Mercury is not at its best here as the changes suggested by Mula will be difficult to accept intellectually. It must learn to change the way it thinks. Jupiter is strong in its own sign, although a Ketu nakshatra will not allow Jupiter to function independently. It creates new situations for Jupiter and connects past lives strongly to its present wisdom. Venus placed here is uncomfortable as Mula is concerned with renunciation and Venus is about enjoying the pleasures of life. Venus brings its past life problems into this life, and to find happiness it needs to deal with these issues. Saturn in Mula can help towards gaining the strength needed for the move towards spiritual discipline, but it has a habit of bringing karmic situations to the forefront whether they need to be faced at this moment or not.

9

THE YOGAS

The concept of yogas is unique to vedic astrology. It is recognised by planetary combinations placed in specific relationships to each other; they indicate the maturity of the soul and provide 'tests' through which the soul is able to develop. Some yogas will ease the way while others will cause difficulties to be overcome, however there are many combinations so here we will concentrate only on those that are associated with the lunar nodes.

Rahu Ketu form two very important yogas in the chart: the Guru Chandala and the Kal Sarpa. The Guru Chandala yoga is usually connected to your basic philosophy (although it may have an impact on other areas as well), while the Kal Sarpa yoga is the most challenging as it affects every area of life. Neither yoga indicates success or lack of it, but the major psychological issues that are likely to come up during your lifetime.

Guru Chandala Yoga

When Jupiter conjuncts either Rahu or Ketu it forms the Guru Chandala yoga. This was once considered a malefic yoga as Rahu Ketu are Chandalas or Outcasts and it promotes an interest in foreign religions or ideas. Jupiter (the guru) is the most benefic of planets, as it can inspire us to reach for high philosophy, religion and an ethical way of life, but its connection with the nodes changes the quality. An interest in different religions or the following of teachers from a foreign caste or society is no longer considered a negative practice, but with this placement you must be wary of meeting corrupt gurus or teachers who are not on the correct path. It is important to see where this yoga is placed on your birth chart. If, for example, Jupiter Rahu are placed in Cancer, the sign of Jupiter's exaltation, it is likely that you would meet an excellent guru although probably from a foreign country. The same may not be true if Rahu and Jupiter were placed in Capricorn, Jupiter's sign of debilitation. Then you would have to learn an important lesson from your association with a foreign guru who may not be totally spiritual or ethical. You should also check the placement of the dispositor. If the it is placed in the 6th, 8th, or 12th houses - the dushtana houses - then the yoga may also manifest its more negative aspects.

Kal Sarpa Yoga

Kal Sarpa yoga is formed when Rahu and Ketu contain between them all the remaining planets in the natal chart. For example if Rahu is 10⁰ Aquarius and Ketu 10⁰ Leo and all the remaining planets are within these degrees, either from Leo to Aquarius or Aquarius to Leo, then it is Kal Sarpa (remember that vedic astrology does not use the outer planets Uranus, Neptune and Pluto). For this yoga to be complete, no planet should conjunct Rahu or Ketu. Some authorities also believe that for the yoga to be properly felt, the planets should be within the Rahu to Ketu axis and not vice versa. That is: if Rahu was 10⁰ Aquarius and Ketu 10⁰ Leo, all the planets must be situated in the signs running from Aquarius to Leo. In this scenario, when Rahu transits over these planets it would effectively eat them up, and its impact would be more acute. In my opinion, planets on either side of the axis relate to a Kal Sarpa yoga and depict a restriction of the planets' energy.

A person with the Kal Sarpa yoga pattern may find that however capable they are, their life is impeded due to past karma. Obstacles are encountered at every junction for inexplicable reasons; important lessons have to be faced, and no amount of effort seems to be rewarded, but in fact the rewards are spiritual rather than material.

Kal means time and *Sarpa* means snake, which together indicates the soul of an individual caught in the snake of time. The snake wraps around the subconscious like a rope pulling tighter and tighter whenever we try to break free of it. The main impact of this yoga is psychological as it is our own negativity holding us back. It does not suggest either success or failure, more the feeling of being caught up in karmic forces so great that they are restrict our destiny. It acts mysteriously, without other indications in the birth chart. An individual may be extremely successful, yet an equally large part of their life remains unfulfilled. Many people with this yoga find half their life in darkness and half in the light of their achievements. A heavy price is now being paid for past karma. Understanding and counteracting the effects of Kal Sarpa yoga requires the person to move towards their higher self. It is important to understand the psychic implications and the inner blocks created by this combination.

Some of the successful people with this yoga are Nelson Mandela, Paul McCartney, and Harrison Ford. Nelson Mandela paid a heavy price for his beliefs;

Paul McCartney, though very successful, will forever be 'one half' of Lennon and McCartney. The perception of failure or lack of success is in the mind of the individual as others may consider them extremely successful.

A Working Example of Kal Sarpa Yoga

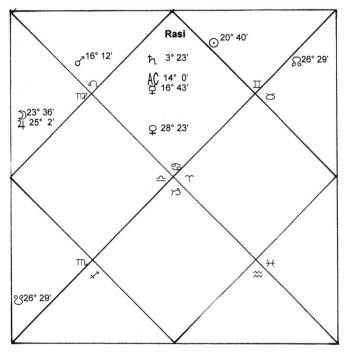

George W. Bush, the 43rd President of the USA
6th July 1946 07:26 EDT (+4:00) New Haven, Connecticut, USA
72W55, 41N18

George W. Bush, the 43rd American President, has Kal Sarpa yoga in his chart. Rahu is 26°30' Taurus, Ketu is 26°30' Scorpio, and all the planets are between Taurus and Scorpio. George W. Bush was elected Governor of Texas for two terms and then became President of the United States of America with a controversially narrow electoral margin. This shows that the Kal Sarpa yoga does not deny success, but it does create obstacles in its path. However, Rahu Ketu are excellent planets for political success. The first thing to note in a Kal Sarpa is the quality of Rahu Ketu. Here both are exalted and Rahu is in the 11th house - the best house for its placement.

The next step is to examine the quality of the Ascendant lord as its strength becomes an excellent counter force for this yoga. Here the Ascendant is Cancer and its ruler (the Moon) is placed in Virgo with the greater benefic (and 9th lord) Jupiter, creating a Gaja Kesari yoga: Gaja means elephant and Kesari is a lion, so this yoga gives the strength of these mighty animals. It is formed by the conjunction or square (Kendra) of Jupiter and the Moon. In this chart the Moon is also waxing, enhancing it further, and is in mutual reception with Mercury, adding to the strength of the horoscope. Mars, the raja yoga karaka for Cancer rising, is placed in Leo and is Vargottama, which means it is in the same sign in both the natal and ninth divisional chart (navamsa). This creates a powerful quality in the chart that is able to fight the restrictions imposed by Kal Sarpa. But George W. Bush still had to face the restrictions this yoga presented. He was born to a successful father and great political lineage, yet his earlier years of life were obscured by bad business deals and an addiction to drugs and alcohol. He was not considered to be successful.

He experienced the Rahu dasha from 15th May 1953. His feelings of restriction, lack of confidence and spiritual dilemma started very young (age 6) and were difficult to manage, yet the quality of Rahu in its exaltation and its placement in Mrigasira nakshatra (ruled by his yoga karaka Mars), protected him through his darkest times. He is fortunate that he has paid the price of Kal Sarpa at an earlier age. Even his election to the presidency was not an easy one, with half the electorate giving him the thumbs down. Although it is difficult to see into the mind of others, the Kal Sarpa yoga suggests that George W. Bush feels this division acutely. Turning to Christianity and spirituality has helped him on his path and, in a similar way, he has to let go the bitterness of the hard fought election or he may create more psychological problems for himself. George W. Bush is successful by all standards, but the problems he has in recognising his success are caused by the Kal Sarpa yoga.

10

THE TIMING OF THE NODAL EXPERIENCE

To feel the full impact of the nodes you need to be in one of the following:

1.　The dasha or sub dasha period of Rahu Ketu - Rahu having an 18-year period and Ketu a 7-year period. The nodes also have sub-periods in the cycles of other planets through which they exercise their power and influence. When any of these life cycles are activated Rahu or Ketu will have control and dictate what is going on.

2.　Experiencing the transit of Rahu Ketu over your planets. The effects of Rahu Ketu in transit are judged according to the planets they conjunct. The Sun and Moon are the most important planets and a transit of Rahu Ketu over these can create unpredictability, which disrupts your life and forces you to transform. This experience is magnified a hundredfold if Rahu Ketu's dasha or sub-dasha is in operation at the same time.

3.　Influence of the eclipses. If eclipses are taking place within 5 degrees of your natal planets it indicates a time of change. Here it is important to remember that the eclipses work on a psychological level so the effects may not be immediately obvious. The eclipse has great influence whether or not it is visible, and if you are in a nodal dasha as well, its influence will be multiplied.

The Vimshottari Dasha System

This is a system of predicting events that is unique to vedic astrology. Vimshottari means 120 – the optimum life-span in the era during which the Vedas were written; *dasha* means direction. Those 120 years were divided into various phases controlled by the nine planets and it is considered that you only experience the full influence of each particular planet - or the nodes - during its dasha (the full name is *mahadasha*). The shorter periods of time within each dasha are called *sub dashas* or *bhuktis*. Moving from one phase into another involves a change in life direction. Whilst the birth chart suggests the passive, past life influences you have brought with you, it is the dasha system that indicates when these issues will become prominent. On analysis of your chart, you will become aware that certain areas of your life run smoothly while others seem troublesome; understanding your dasha pattern will help you to anticipate them and act accordingly.

Rahu Ketu remain passive energies in our charts until we are going through one of their dashas. The length of their cycles are such that most of us will experience either one of the nodes as a dasha ruler in our lifetime. We experience their impacts through their sub dasha too but it is the dashas themselves that give Rahu Ketu their maximum effect. You can use these periods as an opportunity to understand how the shadowy nature of the nodes works in real life. They tend to teach important and serious life lessons, but much can be achieved if you understand and use the energy properly. It can be a wonderfully spiritual experience.

The Bhuktis
Bhuktis are the nine sub-divisions experienced during a mahadasha. Here you must note the relative positions of the bhukti ruler to the dasha ruler: it is not helpful for the bhukti ruler to be in the 6th, 8th or 12th house position from the dasha ruler. The 2nd and 11th houses are good, the 3rd is neutral, and the 5th or 9th house positions are perfect. Planets in *kendras* (1st, 4th, 7th or 10th house) to each other will create some tension but will be generally useful.

Analysing Rahu and Ketu dashas and sub dashas
1.   The placement. Rahu is well placed in the natal chart in the 3rd, 6th, 10th and 11th houses and will give very good results. Ketu in the 12th is good for spiritual development.

2.   The planets they conjunct. The nodes are best placed on their own as they create problems for any planets they partner, but the reverse is not true, for the planets can actually enhance the nodes. Both Rahu and Ketu will take on the hue of any planet they conjunct, so with benefics they are beneficial, but with malefics they can double the negativity. A conjunction of Rahu or Ketu with the ascendant ruler will colour every aspect of your life. The placement of Rahu Ketu with the 5th and 9th house rulers will give great success.

3.   Its dispositor. Rahu and Ketu will act like the planet which rules the sign where they are placed. The strength and weakness of the dispositor plays an important part in this assessment as a debilitated planet will weaken while an exalted planet will strengthen. If the planetary ruler is friends with your ascendant ruler the dasha will give extremely good results, but if the planet is negative for your ascendant ruler the dasha will bring forth issues which increase the negativity. For example, if Rahu is placed in the 9th house in the sign of Aries, its dispositor would be Mars. If Leo was rising, in this example, Mars would be the *rajayoga karaka* or best planet as Leo and Rahu in its dasha will magnify the results. If Virgo was rising, the same Mars would be the ruler of the 3rd and 8th houses and therefore negative. Rahu in Aries would now be placed in the 8th house too and the impact of this dasha would be very different. (You may want to refer back to the Friends and Enemies chart in Chapter Five.)

4.   The nakshatra dispositor. The nakshatra dispositor has to be assessed as in the paragraph above. You will also need to see whether the planet (dispositor) in question is placed in its own nakshatra. This would intensify the psychic energy and make the dasha a very important one from a karmic point of view.

5.   The bhukti (sub dasha) ruler. Placement of the bhukti ruler from the nodes as well as from their dispositors will be crucial in assessing their impact. Planets placed in the 6th, 8th or 12th house from the nodes or their dispositors will create challenges. In a similar way, when you are analysing the nodal bhuktis the relative placement of their and their dispositor's placement from the dasha ruler has to be taken into account. If you were experiencing a Rahu Jupiter dasha and Rahu was in Libra, the position of its dispositor (Venus) from Jupiter will be vital for the final analysis as to how this bhukti will work out. If (in this example) Jupiter were in Capricorn and Venus in Gemini, then Jupiter would be placed in the 4th house from Rahu highlighting home issues. Venus as the dispositor would be in the 9th house from Rahu, which is excellent, but in the 6th house from Jupiter, which is more negative. The negative positioning of Jupiter from Rahu's dispositor would make this dasha much more difficult.

The Rahu Mahadasha - 18 Years

The effects of the Rahu mahadasha largely depends on both its house placement and its dispositor. Rahu is about experiencing life, so during a Rahu dasha you must be conscious of trying to control your ambitions. Rahu recognises no boundaries so beware of building unrealistic expectations as these can bring dissatisfaction and frustration if unfulfilled. Rahu is the mouth of the snake, and the beginning of this dasha can be like putting your head voluntarily into its mouth. You may be stung and the venom is powerful, but you can either work to find an antidote or allow that venom to control you. I find that the beginning and end of a Rahu dasha has to be handled with great care. Karmic influences dominate and it is difficult to judge what kind of reaction they are going to provoke. In fact the influence of the onset of a Rahu dasha can be felt in the last bhukti (sub-division) of the preceding dasha, which is Mars/Moon. As Mars deals with courage and Moon the mind, this dasha usually focuses the mind on your urgent need to fulfil your inner desires. Just as you then start working to fulfil these, you suddenly reach the Rahu period when you are least prepared for its dramatic impact. In such instances I advise my clients to focus carefully on the coming Rahu dasha, feel the changing energy and take time to assimilate it. Instead of over-expressing desires, you have to learn to put them in perspective, and encourage self-discipline and self-knowledge. Treat yourself with care and avoid going into new situations which you know instinctively are not good for you. Vedic astrology gives you foreknowledge of the times of crisis in your life and it is usually best to deal with them with a calm mind and emotional strength. If you know it is going to rain, carry an umbrella!

This could sound a bit depressing and worrying, but the Rahu dasha can be a fantastically successful one for you if Rahu is strong in your chart. The beginning of the dasha is always difficult. The dasha itself is like a roller coaster ride where you are up one moment and down the next. It can be an exciting and exhilarating experience for those who have a taste for life on the edge, but for others it is important to batten down the hatches, secure your seat belt and be prepared for an extreme experience.

At one point during the dasha of Rahu you will have a sub-dasha of Ketu. The karmic axis of your life will be activated and the whole course of your life could change as the dasha and sub-dasha generate the wisdom to make you aware of your karmic limitations and ultimately lead you to your spiritual self and destiny.

A positive Rahu dasha brings success, prosperity, wealth, foreign travels, pilgrimage, higher knowledge, fame and happiness; it has the ability to fulfil your wildest ambitions. A negative Rahu dasha can make you can feel out of control, alone and helpless. There may be many changes in residences, heavy expenditures and mental suffering. The beginning of any Rahu dasha is formidable but as you learn its lessons you move towards a greater equilibrium. If you have a difficult Rahu position, you must allow the spiritual side to dominate. Most of the problems indicated are experienced in a life where desires are indulged without restriction. The difficult house placements then become a blessing in the Rahu dasha as they allow you to access inner knowledge and work with your higher self. There will be many distractions but by keeping your Rahu power in check, you can change its energy from negative to positive. If you feel afraid to let go of your desires remember the first step into the spiritual is always daunting. Take it slowly and you can use the Rahu energy positively.

The Rahu Bhuktis
In Rahu bhuktis the important timings to watch for are Rahu/Rahu, Rahu/Ketu, Rahu/Moon, Rahu/Sun and Rahu/Mars.

Rahu/Rahu: You will feel the Rahu energy immediately as it brings forth a new dimension. Trust your instincts but be realistic and practical. Beware of grand plans which do not have strong base in reality. Rahu can produce a wonderful time for you if it is well placed.

Rahu/Jupiter: This can be very good, but watch out for over-expansion. Jupiter is the planet of increase and Rahu has unparalleled ambition so together they can make you over confident, expand too rapidly, take one risk too many and spend like a king. If you are currently within this dasha, be realistic, especially if you are involved in gambling or the stock markets.

Rahu/Saturn: Saturn is a friend of Rahu so if Jupiter has made you reckless, Saturn will return you to a more realistic path. It teaches discipline and focusing of energies, and provides a reality check whether you like it or not.

Rahu/Mercury: This will produce a good time as Rahu and Mercury are friends. Mercury will help you to analyse your ambitions and give a strong practical base to your life.

Rahu/Ketu: This is the toughest part of the Rahu dasha. It focuses your mind on deeper-rooted soul issues, and is the time when your karmic axis is fully activated. All the issues we have talked about in this book - how the nodes relate to you in your chart, how they affect you on different levels - this is the time that they are really felt. Even those who experienced this dasha at a young age may have found the Rahu Ketu dasha brought problems that now form a permanent part of their psyche. If you have taken time to meditate on the dilemmas of ethics, ambitions and life purpose, then by the end of this dasha - after the feelings of confusion and helplessness have disappeared - your psyche will have changed completely. Ketu will have encouraged the rejection of negative personality traits and re-established a contact with your soul. If you are about to experience this dasha, use this knowledge to spare yourself the angst and heartache and look at life more spiritually. Try to recognise your karmic axis and deal with it. This bhukti can be a profound time for connecting to your past lives and understanding and coming to terms with their issues. (Refer to the chapter on remedial measures at the end of the book.)

Rahu/Venus: Venus is a good friend and guru to Rahu and brings calm after the storms of the Rahu/Ketu dasha. This can be a time for success and achievement - Venus will smooth the way.

Rahu/Sun: This can be difficult because whatever success you achieve, you may still feel unfulfilled or unappreciated. You may find yourself wanting success so badly that it creates a fear of failure within.

Rahu/Moon: Rahu's greatest enemy is the Moon so this is considered the most mentally difficult period, especially if the Moon is placed with Rahu. Rahu Moon will be better than Moon Rahu. Both deal with the subtle self and this can create irrational fears and depression even if well placed in your chart. It is a time to take care of your inner self. By understanding this powerful energy, you can appreciate the dasha, but it is not a good time to explore kundalini or the darker, more mysterious areas of life.

Rahu/Mars: Rahu and Mars are considered enemies. As this is the ending of the Rahu dasha, Mars can bring a sudden urgency to achieve that can test your spiritual resolve and create problems unless it is well placed. The ending of a dasha should always be treated with care and the last month of this period is especially sensitive. It is a time of closure for many aspects of your life so is not a good idea to begin anything new. You are moving from the shadowy Rahu to the expansive and beneficial Jupiter. I find Rahu becomes very compulsive and obsessive in this last part of the dasha, raising its demonic head and taking this last chance to throw temptations in your path and impose its personality on you. Vedic astrology has a clear message about this period: work positively with this energy and be happy with whatever you have right now - because whatever Rahu and Mars are promising you at this moment is an illusion.

The Ketu Mahadasha - 7 Years

Ketu differs from Rahu in that you feel like giving things up rather than experiencing them. You may feel like changing jobs or even moving into a retreat. Most people experience powerful life issues over which they have no control. The Ketu dasha will start the spiritualising process for a soul that is ready for it.

It can also bring immense success, but you need to be aware of the end of the Ketu dasha - the sting in its tail - as it usually takes away what it gave at the beginning. Most people will experience this axis only once and therefore it can bring intense experiences. Ketu can cause great impediments in your path, setting up roadblocks and traffic jams on your journey; it causes pain and wants to change your psyche. You learn to leave the excess baggage of your past karma behind and travel lightly. The dasha will highlight the issues you need to address in this life and encourage the letting go of the past. There is a mystical quality to the Ketu dasha that is like a ritual of fire from which one emerges stronger and more powerful. Ketu is known as *Dhwajah*, a flag, which has the image of flying high above everyone else. Its association with a planet in dignity has the capacity to boost its capabilities for good or ill during its dasha.

Ketu is a wanderer, with no material attachments. Wherever it is placed in a natal chart it gives disenchantment with worldly success. Its aim is for moksha - spiritual realisation. Under its influence you may voluntarily roam the world or choose a life of poverty, but Ketu works with courage on our inner world during its dasha. It strives to conquer the hidden demons that halt our progress on a spiritual level. It delves deeply into the mysteries of life so that the outer crust is destroyed and a new way of thinking, a new direction of life is achieved. Ketu breaks through the mental barriers constructed by past lives and the present birth and seeks a radically different life on a mystical, spiritual level.

The Ketu dasha can bring foreign travels, spiritual journeys, karmic experiences, power, success, wealth and a recognition of your spirituality. It is during this period that we experience the need to explore our past life issues. A positive Ketu dasha makes the connection a lot easier. It helps you to feel comfortable with your past life and able to bring to a close the issues that are no longer relevant. A negative dasha makes closing the door on the past life more challenging as you are more inclined to hold on to your emotional baggage. Facing up to your karma is part of the Ketu experience. You must repay your karmic debt and move on.

The Ketu Bhuktis
Ketu/Ketu: This can be a special period as it is usually the first time that many people become aware of the spiritual side of their nature and a life other than the material trappings they were born to. Many people start studying astrology or understanding karma and past lives at the onset of a Ketu dasha. Ketu may make you wander, perhaps to far-off places in search for your spirituality, leaving traditional views behind. On the negative side Ketu may make you give up what you otherwise treasure, so it is important not to change your life too radically just now. Allow the Ketu energies to manifest naturally. You are moving

towards a new and more spiritual dimension. The journey it is not necessarily about changing jobs, relationships, or anything else in your outer life; the change demanded by Ketu is within your mind.

Ketu/Venus: Although Venus is a friend of Ketu, this period can focus strongly on the relationship element of your chart and bring latent difficulties to the fore. Karmic relationships are highlighted, and many existing relationships may end.

Ketu/Sun: Ketu's most difficult relationship is with the Sun and identity crises over the soul and its direction come to fore. This time can also bring out issues with authority, the father etc. You feel the need to refocus your whole identity.

Ketu/Moon: This is a challenging time for emotions and you may have to deal with some kind of rejection. The relationship with your mother is highlighted and you should watch out for emotional dissatisfaction.

Ketu/Mars: This combination will intensify the Ketu effects. You need to be wary of being too militant about your spirituality but it can positively push you into going the extra step spiritually. The inner churning of Mars can also drive you to do something forceful in the outside world, such as protesting about injustice.

Ketu/Rahu: This is the most formidable part of the Ketu dasha when your karmic axis is fully activated and all the nodal issues become strong and focused. Even those who experience this dasha at a young age will find, when looking back, that it caused problems of a long lasting psychological nature. This dasha churns up your emotions so much that you feel helpless and unable to find answers to the way your life is working, but Rahu will focus on the past life and through these experiences you are able to find new understanding and bring to closure your karmic past. At the end of this dasha your psyche will have changed completely. If you are about to experience this dasha, use this knowledge to spare yourself the angst and heartache. Look at life more spiritually, be honest with yourself and try to recognise your karmic axis. It is a way to connect to your past lives and work out the difficult aspects in your present life. (Refer to the chapter on remedial measures at the end of the book.)

Ketu/Jupiter: Guru Jupiter comes after the Rahu sub dasha to teach Ketu wisdom and guide it towards the next step in spiritual maturity. This can be a time to explore new philosophies while you study and reflect on what happened before.

Ketu/Saturn: Saturn forces you to be practical and face reality, so if your life in the Ketu dasha has been one of search and no focus this period will help you to redefine yourself. It is a time when idealistic ideas will not be enough in themselves and you have to find a way to use them in the reality of life.

Ketu/Mercury: Mercury is a materialistic planet and can encourage Ketu to give up its spirituality, so this is a crucial time. Mercury analyses the impact of the Ketu dasha as it draws to a close, and in my experience the end of the 7-year spiritual process makes you feel like giving up many worldly ties and letting go of things that were precious to you. But act carefully during this time. Watch out for Ketu's sting in the tail.

Rahu Ketu Bhuktis in Other Planets' Dashas

You will experience both Rahu and Ketu bhukti periods in other planetary dashas and you need to see them as mini influences on your karmic axis. The issues produced will be similar to those experienced in the respective nodal dashas, but as the time frame is limited their impact may not be as intense. If you have a difficult nodal axis in your chart, then you have to be careful during these times. To analyse them, study the way the nodes behave in their own dasha times. As the bhukti lords are believed to have a powerful influence on the dasha lords, these short nodal periods can be very intense. Be especially careful at the beginning and ending of the nodal bhuktis.

The Rahu Bhuktis in Other Planetary Dashas:
Sun/Rahu: This can be a time for success as you try to establish your identity.

Moon/Rahu: Rahu increases the fear in your heart and this is a time when unknown phobias may arise for no reason whatsoever. Be careful that an obsessive search for happiness does not have the opposite effect.

Mars/Rahu: Rahu brings shadows into the open world of Mars, so this can be a tough one to manage successfully.

Jupiter/Rahu: As this is the last dasha for Jupiter it would appear to be a good time for expansion, but be aware that the next dasha is of Saturn, the planet of restriction - the need to control the Rahu energy is important.

Saturn/Rahu: Rahu expands and gives a bigger dimension to Saturn's hard work. This can be a good time.

Mercury/Rahu: This is a good period and can bring about accelerated growth. But guard against mental turmoil and fear in the mind.

Venus/Rahu: An excellent time for growth.

The Ketu Bhuktis in Other Planetary Dashas:
Sun/Ketu: This is a challenging period that can lead to an identity crisis and a poor self-image.

Moon/Ketu: This may bring past life fears and guilt to the fore and you may reject yourself emotionally in the mental turmoil.

Mars/Ketu: Ketu will act like Mars enabling you to achieve anything during this powerful time.

Jupiter/Ketu: You can find spirituality through getting in touch with your past life either consciously or subconsciously. For women it may be a difficult time for relationships.

Saturn/Ketu: As Ketu cuts away from the previous life it is a time of introspection and facing up to spiritual reality.

Mercury/Ketu: A time of changing intellectually, but beware: an unsettled mind can make wrong decisions.

Venus/Ketu: This is the last dasha for Venus so be careful you do not reject what you have spent twenty years building up. Relatives may start taking up a lot of your time as you solve or reassess your relationship with the world.

11

TRANSITS

The transits of Rahu Ketu show the changing energies of your karmic connection. As the nodes transit through different signs they raise consciousness over certain issues while finishing the karmic debt over others. Rahu transits show what you are about to experience and Ketu shows where you are letting go.

Rahu is usually a positive transit enhancing the qualities of the planets it contacts, while Ketu shows up your vulnerabilities and where there is work still to be done. Ketu's transit through a house always connects the past life issues to the present. As Rahu Ketu travel in retrograde motion entering all signs from the 30th degree and moving slowly towards the 1st degree, they gradually bring the key issues to a climax. It is like coming into an area of your life shrouded in fog and lacking visibility, and slowly getting accustomed to it by developing special insight. You were born with the nodal axis in certain houses during your lifetime, but the axis retrogrades back to different house areas with a corresponding shift of emphasis. While the birth issues are the most dominant ones, the transiting positions show how you are dealing with them today.

Transits activated through dashas or sub dashas of Rahu Ketu

Let's say Rahu moves into your 1st house (the self) and Ketu into the 7th (of relationships). This gives you an indication of the area where your underlying past life issues have now to be worked out, and Rahu Ketu will be in this position for 18 months. If your main dasha at the time is neither Rahu nor Ketu, then the self/relationship issue will likely remain in the subconscious but never become dynamic. However you may find that when the sub dasha becomes Ketu - half way through the transit - the relationship issues will suddenly break into consciousness.

Transits through the signs and houses

The transits of Rahu Ketu through the houses and signs will also show the areas affected by eclipses at any given time. The eclipses pinpoint the energy escalation in the axis, both creating crises and giving answers. For example, if Rahu Ketu are in Aries and Libra there will be an eclipse if the Sun is in either of those signs at Full or New Moon.

Transits Through the Signs

Rahu Ketu transiting through the signs shows how the axis is working on a more general level. During the 18-month transit through a sign, Rahu or Ketu will each move through three nakshatras for varying periods, so the subtle influences on the nodes change every few months.

Aries/Libra, Libra/Aries

Aries, the first sign of the zodiac, symbolises a birth or rebirth from the primordial source into matter and Rahu transiting here shows the beginning of a new energy. As the node comes in at 30 degrees of Aries, it will take some time before the influence is completed. Rahu in Aries is looking for a new way of life and Mars, its ruler, will give it the courage to express itself. Ketu in Aries tries to reject new ways and clings to the past, so there can be an increase in both stubbornness and risk taking. However Ketu usually emphasises the spirituality of Aries while rejecting the sensuality. During this nodal transit you need to track Mars' transit. If Mars is strong the transit will be positive, but difficult aspects to transiting Mars will create problems with the nodes' progress. During the Aries transit there will be three nakshatras for Rahu to traverse. Firstly Krittika (for the first 2 months), then Bharani (for the next 8 months), and finally Ashwini (for the last 8 months).

Libra is the halfway point of the zodiac and the cosmic cycle. It represents the culmination of our material dreams and the start of our spiritual ones. Ketu's transit there can disturb the fine Libran balance as it emphasises spirituality and questions the issues of relationships, judgement and bi-partisanship. As Ketu moves from the more spiritual nakshatras to the material ones, you may experience dissatisfaction with the way you are progressing spiritually. Rahu in Libra focuses on partnerships but can disturb the Libran balance through obsession and extreme focus. However this is usually a positive transit as Rahu is a friend of Venus, the Libran ruler. Transiting Venus will also assume a strong focus during this time, and as Venus is a fast moving planet, many different aspects of life will be highlighted. If Venus becomes debilitated during this transit, expect a challenging time. If it is exalted, things will be very positive.

The nodes will also be transiting through three nakshatras in Libra: Vishakha (first 6 months), Swati (next 8 months) and Chitra (last 4 months). As Rahu rules Swati its transit will be positive, but Ketu's transit through Swati will increase inner turmoil. You should also observe how Venus and Mars relate to each other during this transit. If they are placed in the 6th, 8th, or 12th house from each other, it can be difficult and would create disturbance. With other easier aspects you can solve your dilemmas harmoniously.

Taurus/Scorpio, Scorpio/Taurus

Rahu is exalted in Taurus and this transit will therefore be a positive experience. Ketu is debilitated in Taurus so it will reject the Taurean qualities related to the practicalities of life (money, food and material comforts). Venus, the ruler of Taurus, is a fast moving planet and changes signs every 25 days, so the quality of Venus in transit will keep changing your experience of the nodes. The nakshatras will also exert their subtle influence, starting with Mrigasira (for the first 4 months), then Rohini (the next 8 months) and finally Krittika (the last 6 months).

Scorpio is a complex and difficult sign but Ketu is exalted here and makes the difficult issues a bit easier. There can be strong karmic experiences. The beginning of the transit will highlight your spiritual involvements, moving more towards the mundane as the transit progresses. Rahu is debilitated in Scorpio and its transit can bring out the darker side of your nature. You must be careful of he company you keep during this time. The nakshatras change from Jyeshta (for the first 8 months), to Anuradha (the next 8 months) and finally to Vishakha (the last 2 months). The health of Mars during this transit will also influence its quality. The changing experience of the axis will be modified by the relationship between transiting Mars and transiting Venus.

Gemini/Sagittarius, Sagittarius/Gemini

Rahu in Gemini is good for technical and intellectual pursuits. It focuses on business and communications. Mercury rules Gemini, so its transits become the focal point of the Rahu expression. Ketu is not comfortable with the analytical Gemini and there will be conflict between the emotions and the rational mind. Mercury is a fast moving planet retrograding three times a year, which can mean there may be as many as five retrogrades to experience during the 18-month nodal transit. These Mercury retrogrades will pull the nodes back to the past and create tension, but this turmoil will bring the best out of you eventually. In Gemini the nodes will transit the nakshatras Punarvasu (for the first 6 months), Ardra (the next 8 months), and Mrigasira (the final 4 months). Ardra is ruled by Rahu so the Rahu transit can be intense.

Ketu is a spiritual warrior in harmony with the Sagittarian impulse of striving to control the lower self to attain the higher. Here Ketu is moving backwards from the more spiritual to the more mundane, so there is a feeling of disappointment at the end of this axis. Rahu in Sagittarius can be positive, bringing out the better part of Rahu's nature, although you must be careful at the end of this transit not to be pulled back into its darker side. Jupiter, the ruler of Sagittarius, is a slow moving planet usually staying in a sign for a year, so the nodes will only experience two different kinds of Jupiter energy. Subtle influences are also felt as the nakshatras change from Uttara Ashadha (for the first 2 months), to Purva Ashadha (the next 8 months), and then Mula (the final 8 months). The nodes transiting Mula should prove the greatest challenge.

Cancer/Capricorn, Capricorn/Cancer

As Cancer is ruled by the emotional Moon, Rahu's transit here can create quite a lot of mental stress. The Moon changes sign every 2½ days and as Rahu's dispositor it has the ability to churn up many issues. The Moon focuses on your heart and your instincts, and you will be in for a turbulent 18 months if you allow these to rule you. Ketu in Cancer shows that emotions will be your vulnerable point and Ketu will reject your emotional needs, so this can be a tough transit. Try to stay calm and don't ignore the work you must do. The nodes will transit through the nakshatras of Ashlesha (for the first 8 months), then Pushya (the next 6 months), and finally Punarvasu (the last 2 months), each bringing its own subtle influence.

Ketu is not comfortable with Capricorn. Saturn, the dispositor, deals with reality and forces Ketu to express its mysticism and idealism practically. There can be scepticism over such 'otherworldly' factors. Rahu in Capricorn feels more at home as Capricorn disciplines the Rahu energy and, in the process, forces you to be more realistic about life. Saturn is the slowest moving planet and will most likely stay in the same sign throughout the entire nodal transit. If Saturn does change sign, expect to see a major shift in energies. The nakshatras Dhanishta (for the first 4 months), Shravana (the next 8 months) and Uttara Phalguni (the final 6 months), will also influence the subconscious.

This axis is probably the toughest one to experience. The relative relationship between the Moon and Saturn keeps changing on a daily basis creating many emotional disturbances. It can seem as if your life is in eclipse through a non-understanding of your own emotional issues. But unless this transit replicates your own birth axis, you will be able to control these issues by remaining aware of the potential.

Leo/Aquarius, Aquarius/Leo

Rahu represents psychological power and Leo physical prowess. This can be a strong transit focusing on power as well as the corruption of power. On the world stage you can see many heads of state change during this transit when they are suddenly faced with darker forces. On a personal level this transit can bring a great rise in your power. Rahu in Leo establishes authority and makes you feel invincible, but Ketu in Leo wants to reject all trappings of power and hide its strengths behind others. During this period you may lack self-confidence in yourself and start feeling that your strengths have become weaknesses. The Sun as the dispositor will focus on a different area of life each month, so there are 18 different ways for this nodal transit to express itself. Be aware of the Sun's ingress into new signs, usually on the 15th of the month. Also the Sun's debilitation (in Libra) and its exaltation (in Aries) will both be experienced, giving their own special meanings. The nakshatras Uttara Phalguni (the first 2 months), Purva Phalguni (the next 8 months) and Magha (the final 8 months), are the subtle influences. Magha is especially difficult as it is ruled by Ketu.

The Ketu transit through Aquarius is good for spiritual discipline and democracy. It is a time when individual personalities are ignored and the majority view of the people is expressed. Public protests against monarchs or government leaders are at their height. (The public mood of hostility towards the British monarchy immediately after the death of Princess Diana - which Queen Elizabeth was urged to publicly address - happened while Ketu was in Aquarius). Rahu in Aquarius will also highlight democracy and people-power, but where Ketu shows protest Rahu activates the acquisition of the democratic power. There is an emphasis on alternative lifestyles in medicine, spirituality etc. New Age agendas become strong. Saturn, ruler of Aquarius, might only change sign once during the transit - if at all. The nakshatras will change from Purva Bhadra (the first 6 months), to Shatabhishak (the next 8 months) and then Dhanishta (the last 4 months), with their corresponding subtle influences. The Rahu-ruled Shatabhishak period is the most disturbed, creating political upheaval and bringing out many dark aspects of life. This axis will be difficult at times and much easier at others, depending a great deal on the Sun's relative position to Saturn. However it is difficult to be totally at ease during this transit.

Virgo/Pisces, Pisces/Virgo

Rahu in Virgo is in dignity. It can be a good time for material success. Mercury the Virgo ruler creates radical shifts in Rahu's demands on our lives as it retrogrades backwards and forwards during the 18-month period. Ketu is not totally at ease with the conformist Virgo and can make you question both your material needs and your position in society. You may decide to give up your material life for a more spiritual one, but only as these needs are highlighted by the changing transit. Remember you may need your security when this transit has ended, so don't burn all your bridges. Special emphasis has to be on the times that Mercury combusts and becomes as invisible as the nodes, which can create undetected tensions in your life. Virgo is a sign of practicality and to deal with this transit efficiently one must use common sense and discipline. The nodes retrograde through nakshatras Chitra (the first 4 months), Hasta (the next 8 months) and then Uttara Phalguni (the last 6 months).

Ketu moves from its preceding and difficult experience in Aries towards a positive and well-placed energy in Pisces. This is the moksha planet in the sign of moksha and there is going to be a desperate need to connect with the spiritual way of life and leave behind money, security and materialism. Rahu feels uncomfortable with the unreality of the Piscean experience but Rahu in a Jupiter-sign has to look beyond what is visible. Jupiter changes sign every year and its position will show how the spirituality will develop. Remember to observe how Jupiter and Mercury are relating to each other. The Virgo-Pisces axis emphasises the polarities of practicality and idealism. It can make people extremely materialistic but then protest and focus on their spirituality.

Transits Through the Houses

Rahu in 1st and Ketu in 7th
This brings out problems concerning your own identity and your close relations with others. You may focus on yourself too much and leave your partner feeling rejected. The area of vulnerability is your relationship, so watch out for being too ambitious or selfish.

Rahu in 2nd and Ketu in 8th
Here Rahu focuses on finances, Ketu on the mysteries of life. Ketu is in the house of death and transformation so you could be making major changes at this time. As these houses are linked to relationships too, there may be changes in that area. Ketu in the 8th can connect to some negativity from the past so be wary of individuals who are not what they appear.

Rahu in 3rd and Ketu in 9th
Rahu transits over the area of self-will while Ketu resides in the house of spirituality. Relationships with siblings and fathers are in focus. There may be real karmic issues with your father and you need to work out the problems and then let them go. This can be a crisis point in your relationship with your father, but can lead to a fundamental change in the way you interact with each other. Generally this can be a wonderful time to let go of the hurts you carry within.

Rahu in 4th and Ketu in 10th

Rahu transiting the 4th house leads to changes in the way you live or a change of residence. As Rahu is a foreigner it may also indicate your travelling away from home. Meanwhile Ketu in the 10th highlights changes in your career, perhaps voluntarily working in a more spiritual area. You may choose to work in an environment more suited to you ideologically, giving up some of the financial rewards of a more material employment, but with the end result of a better type of career. The axis is making you more aware of your home, your emotions and your mother and finishing a cycle of karmic life in your work/career. Focus on your inner needs and let go of your outer ones.

Rahu in 5th and Ketu in 11th

Rahu here will focus on *purva punya* (past life credits), on creativity, good luck and children. This can be a very positive transit indeed. Ketu in the 11th is a good transit too but can make you oblivious to financial reward. You might not work for money as the need for spiritual rewards gets more urgent. You must try to avoid getting obsessive over your children as Rahu could heighten your fears unnecessarily about them.

Rahu in 6th and Ketu in 12th

Rahu in the 6th will give you the ability to deal with your enemies and detractors. It is also the house of disease so be careful of your health. As the 6th house deals with stepfamilies, these can become important in your life at this time. Ketu in the house of moksha is like a hermit and will focus on your spirituality if you are ready for it. Materially it can bring expenses and sexual issues to the fore.

Rahu in 7th and Ketu in 1st

Rahu in the house of Others creates a huge need to experience satisfaction from relationships. The urgency to find this can result in many affairs. If you are without a partnership, this is one of the transits through which you can be sure of meeting a new love or making a more permanent commitment. Meanwhile Ketu in the 1st house brings out personality problems, focusing on the past life baggage you brought into this life. This is a good time to be honest with yourself, shed some complexes and have a change of psychology. You may be physically or emotionally vulnerable so try not to be too self-critical.

Rahu in 8th and Ketu in 2nd:

Rahu transiting this house can be difficult as it embraces transformation and wants to experience the dark forces of nature. This is a time to be disciplined. Rahu may attract people who are negative for you or take you into areas that you are not prepared for. Drug addictions are the most extreme experience of this transit. Ketu in the 2nd could bring up financial issues connected to inheritance. You may even want to let go of your finances and give them all away. Be careful though, you may not be so happy about your largesse once this transit has passed.

Rahu in 9th and Ketu in 3rd

Rahu focuses on paternal relationships, philosophies and good luck. This is positive. Ketu in the house of siblings could activate some karmic issues and bring to the fore differences carried over from previous lives. The 3rd house also deals with your self-will and the practical side of life. You may suddenly become extremely idealistic and impractical, but remember this is just a transit. These may not be the main issues of your life, so keep it all in perspective.

Rahu in 10th and Ketu in 4th

This is a great transit for your professional success, but not such a hot one for your emotional happiness. Rahu enjoys the 10th house and it will show that you are expressing the karma of this life. Ketu in the 4th house creates a feeling of emotional dissatisfaction particularly if you are over focused on material success and ignoring your spiritual needs. This is a transit where you can be extremely successful yet unhappy.

Rahu in 11th and Ketu in 5th

This is very positive for financial gains. Rahu in the 11th can give a great boost to your financial situation. If you are looking for spiritual gains then these can be on offer as well. But in either sphere try to avoid a feeling of dissatisfaction. You may be achieving great financial success but if you feel you are not achieving enough, you can may take one financial risk too many. You can feel dissatisfied regardless of the amount of money you make. Ketu in the 5th can create issues with children that need to be sorted out. You may feel guilty about your relationship with them, either through letting go or holding on. This is a good time to allow your children to develop independently of your influence and not feel that as a rejection to yourself.

Rahu in 12th and Ketu in 6th

Rahu in the house of loss can make your expenses rocket so keep strict control of the finances. Ketu can bring out enemies or detractors from the past. Deal now with the issues they present rather than ignoring them. Stepfamilies are particularly important during this transit. You may not be totally comfortable with them, but you have to deal with them.

Rahu Transiting Planets

Rahu gives a feeling of expansion and experiencing life to its fullest. Rahu's transit over a benefic planet is always a positive one, encouraging the planetary energies towards fruition. But over a malefic planet it can be very negative and you must check the dasha you are experiencing before deciding on its impact and taking calming action. (See the chapter on remedial measures at the end of the book.) Try to avoid living life on the edge or taking too many risks. Transits will pass and a positive attitude during tough times always helps. Rahu's transits usually highlight materialism and this can create problems for those on a spiritual path.

The Sun

Rahu transiting the Sun enhances your feelings of power and it is a time to embrace success and your heightened public image. It highlights most aspects related to the Sun, like the soul, the self, the father, or the highest authority. This is such a positive transit for you, so do try to avoid expressing the negative side of the solar energy - for example displaying autocratic or egoistic behaviour in compensation for fear of losing your success.

The Moon

Rahu's transit over the Moon is a most challenging one. It can throw a shadow over your happiness, creating unreasonable fears or phobias and making you afraid of your own emotions. Try to work with your fears and learn to deal with them. The important fact to remember is that this transit will be at its most intense when it is applying to, rather than separating from, the Moon. You need to be extra careful at that time. But how this transit affects you overall depends a lot on your own birth chart.

Mars

Mars is a malefic planet and Rahu's transit is not always positive. It can encourage you to take extra risks, and be impulsive and fearless in pursuit of power. For this transit to work well, you need to be cautious and careful. If Mars is a positive planet on your own chart, then this transit can enhance the best of its qualities.

Mercury

Rahu's transit over Mercury will be generally positive as the two are good friends. Your speech is more influential and dynamic, and your intellectual and business powers are enhanced. Be careful to avoid the negative sides of this transit which might encourage ambivalence, secrecy and dishonesty. You may become closer to your stepfamilies or even learn about them for the first time.

Jupiter

Rahu transiting Jupiter can be so positive that you may need to control your ability to overdo things. Jupiter is expansive and so is Rahu, and together they can do too much. You may also get involved in foreign religions or meet someone who is not from your own family background. This is also an indication for having children, especially sons.

Venus

As a friend of Venus, Rahu will positively enhance all the Venusian qualities when it transits over it. This can bring marriage, luxuries, relationships, fine clothes and an interest in the finer things of life including music, literature and the theatre. The transit becomes even stronger if Venus is a good planet for you personally, but generally it will change the quality of your life.

Saturn

Rahu transiting Saturn is very challenging. Both are malefics and both have the ability to bring difficulties in your life. This is the time to face karma. If Saturn is a good planet for you, Rahu will improve its good qualities. But the best antidote for this transit is work and discipline. In fact this transit is good for workers in general, as their rights and voice will be recognised in the larger world.

Rahu

Rahu transiting itself activates the karmic axis. It is the start of a new cycle of karmic development when one part of your life's purpose has finished and it is now time to focus on the next one. What this purpose will be is indicated by the position of your natal dispositor in transit. For example: if your natal Rahu is placed in Gemini, then the position of transiting Mercury at the time of your Rahu return will indicate what the next cycle promises.

Ketu

When Rahu transits natal Ketu, the axis is reversed and confusion abounds. You experience issues with friends and family members about which you can do nothing. You try to work with your past life problems but the transit indicates you are only halfway through understanding aspects of your past life issues. You will not be able to get complete or final answers during this transit as it tends to illuminate and obscure at the same time.

Ketu Transiting Planets

Ketu is always asking you to give up, reject, and renounce. As Ketu looks at things more idealistically, its transits can give unrealistic expectation of what you want from life. You may want to reject the signification of the planets it transits (by house and karaka). Ketu highlights your vulnerability and weakness, the very area the soul needs to work with.

Sun

Ketu transiting the Sun will highlight paternal problems. You may find a lack of appreciation from your father however hard you try to please him. It may be a good time to talk and bring these feeling out in the open, as he may not be conscious of his actions. You may also protest against authority of any kind but you can give up your own power in the process. This may not be what you want naturally, so think hard before you act. This transit usually makes it a difficult time at work, as you feel uncomfortable with those in positions of power over you.

Moon

Ketu transiting the Moon is challenging. You may face emotional rejection or you may reject someone yourself. It could open up old wounds that you have been carrying in your psyche and your relationship with your mother will not be easy. The mind can become agitated and restless, you may reject your emotional needs and it is not a good time to make life-changing decisions, especially when Ketu is applying to - rather than separating from - your Moon. However it is a good time for meditation, yoga, searching for your spiritual roots and controlling your emotional desires.

Mars

As Ketu acts like Mars, Ketu transiting this planet can double the Martian influence. It is not a good time to take physical risks and you need to be careful regarding accidents and personal injuries. Your relationship with your brothers could be difficult.

Mercury

Ketu is instinctive and Mercury analytical, so when Ketu transits Mercury it can teach about emotions but overall it can create confusion. This is a time when you are likely to make wrong judgments and decisions. Your relationship with your sisters could be difficult.

Jupiter

Ketu's transit over Jupiter can make you reject many ideas about life that were instilled at birth and you may adopt a new spiritual philosophy entirely. For a woman, this can be a difficult time with your male partner. There may be a distance between you, and you should discuss any feeling of alienation or rejection.

Venus

Ketu's transit over Venus makes you want a simpler life. You find yourself giving up luxuries and comforts and developing more ascetic tastes. This is a critical transit for love and relationships. You are really seeking spiritual love and this can lead you to give up your present relationship for a better imaginary one.

Saturn

Ketu transiting Saturn is tough. You need to proceed with caution. Ketu activates the malefic energy of Saturn, which may cause sudden pressures and unexpected events. It is a time to stay with the familiar and not voluntarily create disruption. You may feel that your work regime is unfair and wish to take a stand against it. Ketu wants you to give up your disciplined approach to life and chase your dreams but that is not always the practical step to take. The repercussions of Ketu transiting Saturn can be felt for a long time. It can lead to complete reassessment of life and your responsibilities within it.

Rahu

When Ketu transits over natal Rahu it momentarily creates confusion. You feel you need to give up your desires and ambitions and take the path of renunciation. As this represents the halfway stage of a karmic struggle, issues are not clear-cut. Relating to the outer life is difficult when you are still embroiled in understanding your inner voice.

Ketu

A Ketu return (Ketu transiting Ketu) signifies the end of one cycle of soul growth. This is a good time to meditate over the lessons learnt during the past 18 years. It is a time for closure, for paying your karmic debts and letting go of your emotional baggage. If you insist in perpetuating the old conditions, you are tying down your soul and not allowing it to mature and grow. The issues you need to leave behind will be indicated by the position of the natal Ketu dispositor. If your natal Ketu is placed in Libra for example, then the transiting position of Venus (the Libran-ruler) at the time of your Ketu return will indicate what part you need to let go.

The Degrees of Conjunction

The influence of the nodes becomes stronger the closer they get to any planets in the sign being transited, reaching an intensity when they are within three degrees. After they have passed the planetary degree, the influence remains but the intensity reduces until they leave the sign. Rahu Ketu transits to planets are usually at their most concentrated during a two-month period.

12

ECLIPSES

Eclipses are always considered to be omens. In ancient civilizations they were portents of doom. In my experience eclipses are indications of a change - for better or worse - but more importantly they indicate the end of one cycle and the beginning of a new one.

Rahu Ketu can cause eclipses and this is one of the main reasons they were regarded with suspicion. To the ancient sages the eclipses, especially solar, meant that the light from the sun had vanished, and the deadly silence and disturbance of birds and animals made them fear that the end was coming. As the dark shadow of the Moon engulfed the Sun, it appeared as if a demon was swallowing it. An eclipse is always a portent for some change to come, a divine warning. The Sun sheds its light for a moment and exposes the shadow of the Moon which is Rahu, and when Rahu is revealed, our hidden side comes to the surface. An unusual aspect of our consciousness is shown, highlighting a different way of life.

The Solar Eclipse
The Solar Eclipse occurs during the New Moon when the Sun is in line with both the Earth and the Moon. From the Earth's point of view, the Moon's shadow falls on the Sun and we are momentarily in darkness. The astrological effect of a Solar Eclipse lasts for the same amount of time in years as the eclipse took in minutes. For example if the eclipse lasted for two minutes, then the effect of the eclipse will last for two years. What that means in practice is that the actual zodiac degree of the eclipse remains sensitive to planets transiting or aspecting it for a period of two years. Any one of these future movements has the ability to activate the promise of the eclipse. The Moon will cross the eclipse point every month and the Sun yearly, but the greatest impact will be felt when

malefics like Saturn or Mars act as a trigger. It is important to remember that the eclipse itself remains a passive indication for events to occur, not the outcome itself. This misunderstanding leads to many wrong predictions being made when people expect events to happen on the day of an eclipse itself, which creates a lot of fear about observing or experiencing eclipses. In fact as an astrologer, it is your work to observe eclipses and their impact, as this helps in the true understanding of the nodal impact.

The Lunar Eclipse

The impact of a Lunar Eclipse is felt immediately. It does not have the long period of the Solar Eclipse, and it creates a greater disturbance in your feelings, which is felt instantly. The Lunar Eclipse highlights a specific event, creates a situation and lets you deal with it, and it usually all happens within the month. Astrologically I use Lunar Eclipses to give me immediate indications of an event, whereas I tend to track the Solar Eclipse degrees over a few years. As we experience two sets of solar and lunar eclipses at either ends of the year, there are always new energy points being created in the chart. Most eclipses do not effect people directly, and I use them mainly for world events. Nevertheless I remain aware if these points are connecting to my own chart or those of my clients.

Impact of Eclipses on the Natal Chart

Classically, only the impact of an eclipse on the Sun, Moon and Ascendant were considered on the natal chart, but in my experience any planet within 5° of an eclipse will feel its influence. The main effect is on the psyche, which in turn encourages you to take steps to change the physical reality. The Solar eclipse highlights a specific area of your life and brings it into your consciousness. This can create great opportunities or play havoc - it can be either good or bad. The natal Sun, representing the soul, goes through a type of rebirth when touched by an eclipse. If an eclipse is near your Ascendant or its ruler, it indicates a complete transformation in your life. The Moon and Mercury are significators of the mind and intellect, and any influence on them creates an indelible impression. Eclipses on other planets usually have an impact on the houses they rule in your chart: for example, if Venus ruled your 4th and 9th houses then an eclipse (on Venus) would highlight relationship issues in your home or with your father.

Looking at the pattern of eclipses over the next 18 years (refer to table at the end of this chapter), you can see that the solar eclipses tend to miss out signs. There are no solar eclipses in Libra until 2012. The transforming energies are concentrated in Scorpio, Virgo and Pisces up to that time. If you have natal planets within 5⁰ of the eclipse degree you will experience the impact on the houses ruled by the planets and the planets' significators.

Eclipse Premonitions

Eclipses forewarn you of future events. Looking at the chart of a given eclipse should give you an inkling as to what is going to happen. The world is a large place and you may not be interested in many of the events that are happening, but if you are studying or specializing in certain geographical areas, the eclipses are an excellent predictive guide. Studying the effect of an eclipse after the event can also be a very powerful tool to help you in future guidance.

To study an eclipse chart, you must relate it to a person or an event. For example if you are interested in a coming presidential election, go to the list of coming eclipses - usually the solar eclipses - and compare them to the natal charts of the presidential candidates. This will give you an immediate and clear indication of the likely effect. I do some work in the financial markets, so here is an example I noted of an eclipse in action.

NASDAQ Meltdown - Solar Eclipse 5th February 2000

In 2000, when NASDAQ was defining the new economy and stock market prices were riding high, I was asked about the future of this organisation. One of the methods I used was to look at the eclipse of the moment. These dizzying heights reminded me of Rahu and its ability to bring unparalleled success, although it always has the ability to bring you down to earth as well. When you ride the demon Rahu, you must expect a real roller-coaster of a ride.

In New York the time of this eclipse was just before sunrise, so it was not visible in the sky. In fact it was technically a partial solar eclipse and visible only in the area of Antarctica. The chart for the eclipse (in New York) showed many planets, including the eclipse itself, in the 12th house, which is of course connected with loss, and this was clearly indicating that many people were going to experience a loss. But was it going to be financial? Jupiter ruled both the 2nd and 11th houses of money and profit. Jupiter was also going to make a dramatic zodiac conjunction with Saturn a few months later that year on 28th May and was placed (on this chart) with Saturn, the ruler of the 12th house. When Aquarius is the Ascendant, Saturn rules both the 1st house of self and the 12th of loss. The 3rd is the house of self will and I felt this combination was going to create a problem caused by the stubbornness of some people. The ascendant ruler Saturn, at 16⁰ Aries, was moving towards its point of debilitation (20⁰), which it would reach on March 17th. The eclipse was clearly indicating that investors should be careful during that time - the devastation Saturn brings usually lasts for some time.

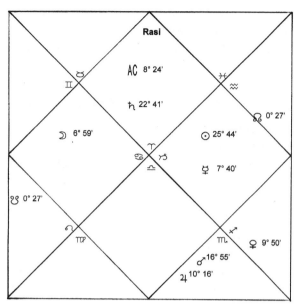

Nasdaq Natal Chart 8th February 1971
10.00 am, Wall Street, NY, USA
74W0 40N42

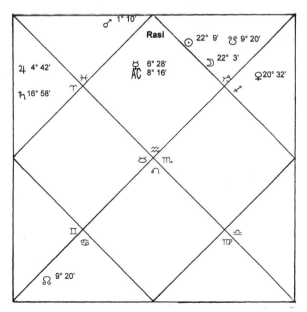

Nasdaq Natal Chart 5th February 2000
07.50 am, Wall Street, NY, USA
74W0 40N42

This eclipse was all the more important as it was near the NASDAQ birth date. The eclipse chart itself was showing all the indications of a major loss but connecting it to the NASDAQ chart further indicated what was going to happen.

ECLIPSE DATES FOR THE NEXT 18 YEARS

Date	Sign	Nakshatra	Type
21/06/2001	06 Gemini 18	Mrigasira	Solar
05/07/2001	19 Sag 46	Purva Ashadha	Lunar
14/12/2001	29 Scorpio 04	Jyeshta	Solar-Gandanta & Sakranti
05/05/2002	11 Scorpio 11	Anuradha	Lunar
10/06/2002	26 Taurus 01	Mrigasira	Solar
24/06/2002	09 Sag 18	Mula	Lunar
20/11/2002	03 Taurus 40	Krittika	Lunar
04/12/2002	18 Scorpio 05	Jyeshta	Solar
16/05/2003	00 Scorpio 59	Vishakha	Lunar-Moon DB Sakranti
31/05/2003	15 Taurus 25	Rohini	Solar
09/11/2003	22 Aries 19	Bharani	Lunar
23/11/2003	07 Scorpio 19	Anuradha	Solar
19/04/2004	05 Aries 55	Ashwini	Solar
04/05/2004	20 Libra 47	Bharani	Lunar
14/10/2004	27 Virgo 11	Chitra	Solar
28/10/2004	11 Aries 07	Ashwini	Lunar
08/04/2005	25 Pisces 11	Revati	Solar
24/04/2005	10 Libra 23	Swati	Lunar
03/10/2005	16 Virgo 23	Hasta	Solar
17/10/2005	00 Aries 17	Ashwini	Lunar- Gandanta & Sakranti
14/03/2006	00 Virgo 19	Uttara Phalguni	Lunar- Sakranti
29/03/2006	14 Pisces 38	Uttara Bhadra	Solar
07/09/2006	21 Aqua 04	Purva Bhadra	Lunar
22/09/2006	05 Virgo 23	Uttara Phalguni	Solar

03/03/2007	19 Leo 02	Purva Phalguni	Lunar
19/03/2007	04 Pisces 09	Uttara Bhadra	Solar
28/08/2007	10 Aqua 48	Shatabhishak	Lunar
11/09/2007	24 Leo 26	Purva Phalguni	Solar
07/02/2008	23 Capri 46	Dhanishta	Solar
21/02/2008	07 Leo 54	Magha	Lunar
01/08/2008	15 Cancer 33	Pushya	Solar
16/08/2008	00 Aqua 21	Dhanishta	Lunar- Sakranti
26/01/2009	12 Capri 31	Shravana	Solar
09/02/2009	27 Cancer 00	Ashlesha	Lunar
07/07/2009	21 Sag 25	Purva Ashadha	Lunar
22/07/2009	05 Cancer 27	Pushya	Solar
06/08/2009	19 Capri 43	Shravana	Lunar
31/12/2009	16 Gemini 15	Ardra	Lunar
15/01/2010	01 Capri 01	Uttara Ashadha	Solar
26/06/2010	10 Sag 46	Mula	Lunar
11/07/2010	25 Gemini 23	Punarvasu	Solar
21/12/2010	05 Gemini 20	Mrigasira	Lunar
04/01/2011	19 Sag 38	Purva Ashadha	Solar
01/06/2011	17 Taurus 01	Rohini	Solar
15/06/2011	00 Sag 22	Mula	Lunar
			Gandanta &
			Sakranti
01/07/2011	15 Gemini 10	Ardra	Solar
25/11/2011	08 Scorpio 36	Anuradha	Solar
10/12/2011	24 Taurus 09	Mrigasira	Lunar
20/05/2012	06 Taurus 19	Krittika	Solar
04/06/2012	20 Scorpio 12	Jyeshta	Lunar
13/11/2012	27 Libra 55	Vishakha	Solar
28/11/2012	12 Taurus 44	Rohini	Lunar
25/04/2013	11 Libra 44	Swati	Lunar
10/05/2013	25 Aries 29	Bharani	Solar
25/05/2013	10 Scorpio 05	Anuradha	Lunar

18/10/2013	01 Aries 43	Anuradha	Lunar
03/11/2013	17 Libra 13	Swati	Solar
15/04/2014	01 Libra 47	Chitra	Lunar
29/04/2014	14 Aries 48	Bharani	Solar
08/10/2014	21 Pisces 02	Revati	Lunar
23/10/2014	06 Libra 21	Chitra	Solar- Sun DB
20/03/2015	05 Pisces 24	Uttara Bhadra	Solar
04/04/2015	20 Virgo 20	Hasta	Lunar
13/09/2015	26 Leo 07	Purva Phalguni	Solar
28/09/2015	10 Pisces 36	Uttara Bhadra	Lunar
09/03/2016	24 Aqua 51	Shatabhishak	Solar
23/03/2016	09 Virgo 12	Uttara Phalguni	Lunar
01/09/2016	15 Leo 16	Purva Phalguni	Solar
16/09/2016	00 Pisces 14	Uttara Bhadra	Lunar- Sakranti
11/02/2017	28 Cancer 23	Ashlesha	Lunar
26/02/2017	14 Aqua 06	Shatabhishak	Solar
07/08/2017	21 Capri 20	Shravana	Lunar
21/08/2017	04 Leo 47	Magha	Solar
31/01/2018	17 Cancer 31	Ashlesha	Lunar
15/02/2018	03 Aqua 01	Dhanishta	Solar
13/07/2018	26 Gemini 35	Punarvasu	Solar
27/07/2018	10 Capri 38	Shravana	Lunar
11/08/2018	24 Cancer 35	Ashlesha	Solar
06/01/2019	21 Sag 19	Purva Ashadha	Solar
21/01/2019	06 Cancer 44	Pushya	Lunar
02/07/2019	16 Gemini 30	Ardra	Solar
16/07/2019	29 Sag 56	Uttara Ashadha	Lunar- Sakranti
26/12/2019	09 Sag 59	Mula	Solar

DB = debilitated

Sakranti - The solar ingress

Sakranti is the moment when the Sun moves into the next zodiac sign and its timing heightens the occult significations. An eclipse at Sakranti shows a huge shift in consciousness.

Gandanta

Gandanta is a special energy point dealing with the maturity of the soul. Specifically it is the last 48 minutes of the last degree of the signs of Cancer, Scorpio and Pisces, and the first 48 minutes of the first degree of the signs of Leo, Sagittarius and Pisces. An eclipse at this point is an intense experience reflecting a shift in the universal consciousness. It indicates a major change in the psychology of an individual if the eclipse connects directly to any natal planets.

Debilitated

I have only listed the Sun or Moon when they are moving towards their debilitation points. The Sun is debilitated at 10^0 Libra and the Moon at 3^0 Scorpio. Debilitated eclipses can give negative effects.

Eclipse conjunctions

To understand the impact of eclipses in your chart, refer again to the chapter on transits and see how the transits effect your houses and planets. If an eclipse is connecting to a specific planet you can expect a magnified impact on the houses the planet rules.

Visibility of eclipses

The visibility of the eclipse gives a divine indication of change, especially if the eclipse is closely conjunct one of your natal planets or your ascendant degree. If this is a Rahu eclipse then you will experience change through expansion and experience of life. If it is a Ketu eclipse it will indicate the letting go of past life influences. Eclipses seem to repeat themselves, forming similar aspects by opposition and conjunction. For example the great Solar eclipse of 11th August 1999 and the Solar eclipse of 5th Feb 2000, were in opposition to each other.

Using the eclipse energy positively

The ancient sages felt that eclipses were a time for the initiation of meditation and learning. They were never used to start material events. It is not a good idea to get married, move house or begin a new project on an eclipse as the day is full of mystical significations and its connection with the karmic impulses can create situations outside human control. The eclipse energies affect your astral body and you may become aware of a spiralling energy connected to disturbances in the Earth's electromagnetic field; this can affect your choices and your ability to make decisions.

The sages also told us never to watch the eclipse. In India, if an eclipse was visible, people would throw away water believing it to be infused with psychic energy. Not every soul is able to cope with this energy, and it is a good idea to avoid planning a hectic schedule and if possible to fast and not consume alcohol. If you find it difficult to fast try being vegetarian for the day. However as an astrologer, I feel it is necessary for us to observe the impact of an eclipse or it will not be possible to analyse and write about its effects. I always note the coming eclipse days in my diary at the start of each year. They are special times and I try to keep the day as spiritual as possible.

13

HEALING YOUR NODAL CRISIS - REMEDIAL MEASURES

Vedic astrology attaches great importance to remedial measures. While your birth chart may suggest certain problems or crises, you still have the ability to change these negatives into positives – it's up to you. The reasoning behind the remedial measures is to encourage you to accept your limitations, understand your weaknesses, and then start working to improve them. If the mind accepts, forgives, and moves on, many of these issues never reach a crisis point. But we are only human and are loath to give up on what we cannot have. Sometimes we are aware that things are not good for us, but we cling on, preferring the familiar to the unknown.

Issues created by the nodes are usually psychic or mental in their nature, dealing with the subconscious and its connection with the conscious. The nodes reveal our limitations and how we struggle with them. The mind can never usually be still and when the nodes are negative it increases the disturbance. There may be psychic wounds that are exacerbated at this time, so the remedies are to clear our psychic fields. This is achieved through yoga, meditation, mantras and pranayama (correct breathing).

Yoga
Hatha yoga and its asanas (postures) allow you to develop your body in preparation for the connection of mind, body and soul. There are many beginner books on this subject, but it is always better to find a good teacher in your area from whom you can learn directly.

Pranayama
Prana is usually described as the breath, but this is a simplistic explanation. Prana is the life force that connects our physical bodies with higher forces and

Yama means practice. Prana and mind are intimately linked as any disturbance to our pranic force will automatically create a disturbance in the mind. Prana is the force that remains with us during different lifetimes as the manifestation of our soul. When we are born, the prana enters our body bringing with it consciousness from previous lives, and it leaves when we die. Any disturbance of the nodes affects our soul and our prana. The best way to work with the nodal upsets is through pranayama.

The left nostril is known as the Chandra (Moon) nadi, and the right nostril is known as the Surya (Sun) nadi. When your breath flows primarily through the right nostril it heats and activates, while if it flows through the left nostril it is cooling or calming. The nadis are subtle veins within your body that connect to the base of your spine. The flow of breath not only sustains you physically but is also responsible for your psychic health. As Rahu Ketu effect the psyche, any crisis they create will immediately be reflected in your breath. Here are some simple yogic breathing practices you can do to harmonise your psyche. Ideally they should be done after the asanas:

General relaxation
Most people breathe wrongly. Relax. Follow the flow of your breath and allow it to move freely. Always breathe through your nostrils. Feel the breath flowing in through your lungs down to your abdomen. Then breathe out slowly. At no time you should be putting any stress on yourself. Your breath should become a natural flowing movement. Repeat this 12 times.

Nadi Sodhana Pranayama (psychic body purification)
Sit in a lotus position (or cross legged if this is difficult). Relax your body.

Hold the fingers of your right hand in front of your face. Place your index and middle finger on the middle of your brow, between the eyebrows. The thumb and the ring finger will control the flow of your breath.

Close your right nostril with the thumb and breathe in and out gently through the left nostril. Do this 5 times.

Close the left nostril with your ring finger. Breathe in and out through the right nostril. Do this 5 times.

Release both the nostrils and breathe in and out from both nostrils 5 times. This sequence is one round. Begin with 3 rounds and progress to 12 rounds. After practicing the nadi shodhana for few weeks you can progress to:

Alternate nostril breathing
Follow the first three steps as before and then:

Close your right nostril with the thumb and breathe in gently through the left nostril. Close the left nostril with your ring finger and breathe out from the right nostril. Breathe in through your right nostril and breathe out through the left, using your fingers to regulate the breath. Do this sequence 3 times and progress to 12.

Meditation
To meditate properly, you need to be in a calm quiet room. Trying to slow down your thoughts does not come easily. If you start your meditation by using mantras and then visualise the yantras or the deities of the nodes, you will gradually quieten your mind. Try to meditate for a few minutes to start with, and then increase the time slowly. At first you will feel restless and many thoughts will disturb your meditation. Allow them to enter your subconscious, do not struggle with them. Let them also leave your consciousness as if they are passing clouds floating through the sky. You will soon find your thoughts become less intrusive. The important thing is not to give up the practice. It usually takes about 40 days to master the beginning of meditation.

The Deities
You can have a visual representative of these when you need to work with your nodes. While you can pray to these deities every day, they also have special days in the lunar month. The day to pray to Ganesha (Ketu) is Chathurti, the 4th day of the waxing or waning Moon phase. Ganesha has a special festival called Ganesha Chathurthi. This is usually at the end of August or beginning of September on the 4th day of the waxing Moon phase after the Sun enters Leo. The day to pray to Durga (Rahu) is Navami, the 9th day of the waxing or waning phase of the Moon. Durga Pooja is a special festival for Durga on the 6th, 7th, 8th, 9th and 10th days of the waxing Moon phase after the Sun has entered Virgo (between 15th September and 15th October).

Yantras
Yantra is derived from the Sanskrit word Y means meditation, *an* means the soul, and *tra* to protect or support. Yantras are mystical diagrams made up of numbers, written in Sanskrit, that reveal a hidden form or subtle inner structure. They comprise not only a numerical structure but also connect to the subconscious. All yantras are psychological symbols or numbers that reveal the inner state of the human psyche. Each yantra becomes the dwelling of the energy

it represents, so a Rahu yantra would represent an abstract image to help in your meditation. It will become especially energised if you chant the appropriate mantra while looking at the yantra. On a subtle level it allows you to understand the hidden aspects of Rahu Ketu. As the nodes are shadows, their yantras become powerful tools in understanding their mystical force.

Mantras

Mantras are sacred sounds. *Mana* means the mind and again *tra* means protection. Mantras are a collection of words which become sacred when intoned in a specific way. By repeating these sounds daily for a specified number of times, you build up a positive energy field around you and protect your mind.

When Rahu Ketu aggravate your subconscious, repeating the mantras allows you to calm your mind and find peace. Mantras should never be undertaken lightly. To benefit you must practice them with concentration, dedication and reverence. Each mantra should be repeated a minimum of 12 times, and you can try to increase the repetitions to 108 times. The best time for saying a mantra is the first thing in the morning or in the evening. I try to do mantras on a long journey, maybe travelling to and from work. Beginners usually say mantras aloud, but it is best to practice them silently. You should try to do mantras for a minimum of 40 days, but the longer you practice them the greater the results. Benefits from repeating these sacred sounds are psychological and they will help create a psychic protection around you.

Rahu Planetary Mantra:
OM Bhram Bhreem Bhroom Sah Rahuve Namah

Rahu Beeja (seed, or short) Mantra:
Ram Rahuve Namah.

Ketu Planetary Mantra:
OM Tram Treem Traum Sah Ketuve Namah

Ketu Beeja (seed) Mantra:
Kem Ketuve Namah

You should practice either a Rahu or a Ketu mantra, then choose between the planetary mantra or the beeja mantra. Chose the mantra of the node that is aggravating you, for example if it is placed in 1st, 2nd, 4th, 5th, 7th,8th, 9th or 12th house of your chart or conjunct a personal planet or the ascendant ruler. Rahu and Ketu conjunct the Moon or Mercury create much psychic disturbance and the mantras will help you deal with this. Do not expect instant results. You need to work with it.

A Special Spiritual Retreat

To keep a healthy psychic body try to visit a special retreat at least once a year. A weekend spent in a retreat practising yoga and meditation is a huge treat as well as being food for the soul. If it is not possible for you to go away, practice at home by allowing your body to withdraw from all sensation. Have a television-free day. Be silent for this special day. Allow yourself to fast or eat simple vegetarian food. Communicate with nature. Try not to read, but if you must, read up on philosophy or higher thinking.

Gems

The gem stone for Rahu is Hessonite and for Ketu is Cats Eye. I usually advise against wearing gems for the nodes as they can seriously disturb your psychic fields and your astral body can be affected. The Sun's kinetic rays change their energy though gems and affect your psychic body in this way. Unless you are 100% sure that you are doing the right thing, I would avoid wearing the nodal gems.

14

CONFRONTING YOUR NODES
THE FINAL ANALYSIS

The placement of Rahu Ketu represent the issues we struggle to achieve or overcome on the mental level. They include our fears, phobias and guilt, together with our need for success. There are past life issues we must release and others we need to work out. Our ultimate goal is spiritual realisation, and Rahu Ketu promise this success if only we can trust their influence.

While analysing the nodes for yourself or for others, I would advise extreme caution and sensitivity. Deep-rooted issues can be revealed and the idea of analysing the chart is to help people understand themselves, not aggravate their nodal crisis. The nodes throw up many issues that accentuate our vulnerabilities and while it is important to examine and discuss them, you need to tread carefully. However difficult the issue, try to give hope. I suggest you work one step at a time. Bringing out deeply buried material from the psyche should be a slow, releasing process, like a kundalini rising. If it is too fast the kundalini gets out of control. It is also important to analyse the whole chart first in order to see how the nodal issues work with the rest of the personality. At the end of the nodal analysis, always guide clients towards remedial work as this will support them in their journey.

I am using Steven Spielberg, the Hollywood director and producer, as a case example. He is famous for unusual films like 'Jaws', 'ET', 'Poltergeist', 'Aracnophobia', 'Close Encounters of the Third Kind', 'Schindler's List' among many others. He created excitement and took people right to the edge through his movies but says he has never been motivated by money or success - he just wanted to make movies. Rahu always signifies addictions, excitement and fear and his chart illustrates beautifully how the Rahu energy can be used in a constructive way. Although he often went against tradition and social opinion, his chart exemplifies the way the nodes can inspire us when we confront up to our fears and limitations. As we are focusing on the nodes in the following analysis, we will be ignoring other aspects of the chart, but by taking the interpretation step by step I hope you will also gain an insight into your own issues.

Step One - The Basics
The Rasi (Natal) Chart

• Rahu is at 17°43' Taurus and exalted. It is placed in the 12th house and in the nakshatra of Rohini ruled by the Moon.

• Ketu is at 17°43' Scorpio and exalted. It is placed in the 6th house in the nakshatra of Jyeshta ruled by Mercury. (I have used Mean nodes. The True node position would be 18°36'. This does not change nakshatra, house or navamsha positions).

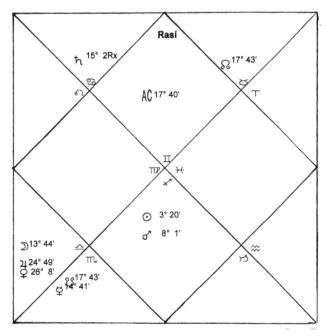

Steven Spielberg - Natal Chart
Born at 18.16 hours EDT, 18 December 1946, Cincinnati, Ohio, USA.
(84W27 39N09)
Source - birth certificate

• As the nodes act like their dispositors, the positions of Venus and Mars are important. Venus is at 26°8' Libra - its own sign. Mars is at 8°1' Sagittarius - a friend's sign. Mars is also in the nakshatra of Mula ruled by Ketu so it is doubly influenced by Ketu being ruled by it and in its nakshatra.

• The nakshatra rulers, the Moon and Mercury are also placed in nakshatras ruled by the nodes.

• The Ascendant is 17°40' Gemini in the nakshatra of Ardra ruled by Ketu.

• The Ascendant ruler Mercury is placed at 14°41' Scorpio conjunct Ketu. It is in the mouth of Ketu.

• The Sun is at 3°20' Sagittarius in the nakshatra of Mula ruled by Ketu.

• The Moon is at 13°44' Libra in the nakshatra of Swati ruled by Rahu.

• The first dasha of Steven Spielberg's life would be Rahu.

The Navamsha Chart
The Rahu Ketu axis is placed in the 4th-10th house axis. Rahu is in Gemini and Ketu in Sagittarius. Mars is conjunct Rahu in Gemini. Mercury is vargotamma - in the same sign in rasi and navamsha.

Dashas
• Rahu from birth until 3rd June 1955.

• Ketu from 3rd June 2007 for 7 years.

Transits
• Nodal returns at ages18, 36, 54, 72 and 90 years. These are all turning points in life.

• Rahu transit over Ascendant at ages 1, 19, 37, 55, 73 and 91years - positive energy.

• Ketu transit over Ascendant at ages 10, 28, 46, 64 and 82 years - vulnerable times.

From this summary, you can see how strongly Spielberg is influenced by the nodes.

Step Two - The Ascendant

The ascendant signifies how you will handle the influence of the nodes, so should always be considered along with its ruler. Steven Spielberg's ascendant is 17°40' Gemini and placed in the nakshatra of Ardra ruled by Rahu. The overall influence of Ardra represents the duality of Gemini: the lust for immortality represented by Rahu, the duality of mind and intellect by Mercury. Both of these energies can be used to enhance the world or destroy it. Spielberg was ambitious to direct films from a very young age, and by 12 he had written and made his own self-funded film. He was expressing the qualities of Rahu in seeking to make a mark on the world. Film is also a world of illusion and shadows - aspects of the Rahu character. Acting and directing is an intellectual exercise and the ascendant ruler Mercury is placed in Scorpio, in the mouth of the snake. As Mercury takes on the personality of the planet it conjuncts, here it takes on the nodal axis. Rahu Ketu were demons among the godly planets and sitting on the tail of Ketu is like riding the devil - a difficult experience for a child. There can be a feeling of being out of control and alienated. Spielberg's father's family came from Russia and his mother's from Poland, so he often felt a resident alien growing up in post war America.

Mercury is also vargotamma. It is in the same zodiac sign in both rasi and navamsha (9th division) which is important as the navamsha chart indicates how much we will achieve of our potential in this lifetime. Vargottamma planets become extremely powerful. Placed in a fixed sign (Scorpio) it suggests great durability and strength and helps the changeable Mercury to be more grounded.

Spielberg felt a strong attachment to his Jewish roots but was at the same time ashamed of them. He hated the fact that he was different from the other children in the gentile areas where his family usually lived, and often felt he didn't fit in. This rejection of one's roots and the guilt attached are expressions of the ascendant ruler being conjunct Ketu. Ketu rejects and holds guilt within itself and sometimes the only way to deal with these painful feelings is to totally cut away from one's roots. It was only with the making of 'Schindler's List' (1993) that Spielberg addressed the problems buried deep within his psyche. After this film he said that his previous shame of being a Jew had now turned to pride. He had always felt angry about the anti-Semitic behaviour he had experienced in the past and was ashamed because he hadn't fought back and had kept his feelings bottled inside. The strong influence of the nodes on his Ascendant and its ruler show the feeling of alienation.

The Ascendant ruler placed in the 6th house of struggles and competition always makes a person feel that they must continually fight battles, and the Ketu conjunction makes it more so. As a child Steven Spielberg was often picked on at school as a nerd and a wimp, Ketu highlighting his feelings of inadequacy. His strength lay in psychological rather than physical warfare but these inadequacies created a strong inner person and an intuitive personality. The 6th is also the house of health and the Ascendant ruler placed there usually indicates poor health. Ketu deals with cutting away (Rahu Ketu were cut into two in their myth) so some people experience this through surgical operations. The body areas ruled by the 6th house are the kidneys and the intestines. Steven Spielberg has had a kidney removed and is generally considered to suffer from poor health. Ketu in the 6th can make diseases difficult to diagnose but it also gives the ability to fight back.

Step Three - The House Axis

The house axis reveals the area where the conflict between our past life karmas and present desires will be fought out. For Spielberg Rahu is placed in the 12th house and Ketu in the 6th. This axis appears in the charts of many creative actors, writers and directors. The 6th house Ketu reflects the struggles he brought into life - being born Jewish at the end of the 2nd World War with all the complex emotions that involved. The 6th is also the house of enemies, of feeling part of a highly competitive world, and Ketu in the 6th will bring unusual enemies and the will to conquer them. Rahu in the 12th connects to the house of imagination. In any house axis one of the nodes is negatively placed and in Spielberg's chart it is Rahu in the 12th that is the more challenging placement. This is decided by observing which sign rules the 12th house and the position of its dispositor (Step Two). This 12th /6th axis indicates that he was meant to understand the lessons of the 12th house in this life, which represent loss, endings, expenses, sexual pleasures and enlightenment. On one level the 12th house reflects hidden indulgences through extravagance or sexual activities, but on another it represents the highest achievement that the soul can experience: enlightenment and the breaking away from the cycles of life and death. Spielberg used the Rahu secrecy to connect to a vivid imagination - his ideas were completely different from anything seen before. The aspect of loss might also have shown in not appreciating himself enough. The 12th is connected with confinement and he used this energy by creating a world of illusion as a director and producer - a behind-the-scenes person. He will never be completely comfortable in the limelight.

Ketu in the sixth house creates powerful enemies, real or imagined. Anyone working in Hollywood would have to face stiff competition from other studios and film directors, but Spielberg was not appreciated by Hollywood society and received no accolades from his peers for a long time. In many ways he would have felt rejected by them, and even now Hollywood confers reluctant admiration on their most successful son. The 6th house might also manifest in sudden illnesses which block one's path, and his health has always been delicate.

Step Four - The Signs

The zodiac signs in which the karmic axis is placed shows how the issues represented by the axis are worked out. Will they be strengthened or weakened? Spielberg's nodes are placed in their exalted signs of Taurus and Scorpio, which suggests that the issues represented by the 12th-6th axis will be worked out to the optimum and the signs will help guide the nodes in expressing themselves in a positive manner. For example, the darker 12th house issues of sexuality, loss and confinement are creatively expressed by Rahu in Taurus; Spielberg has put these energies to practical use by making imaginary worlds into something concrete. The Taurean qualities also help to check Rahu's immense ambition, while Venus has influenced its friend to express its desires properly. Rahu will be creative, disciplined and work towards success.

Ketu in Scorpio is exalted and Ketu acts like Mars, the ruler of Scorpio. Scorpio is a complex and difficult sign but Ketu understands the complexities and deeper mysteries of life. As the 6th house connects to Ketu and Scorpio, the exaltation has helped Steven overcome his enemies and not be oppressed by conditions at birth. If Ketu had not been exalted, he may never have come to terms with his ancestral heritage. Ketu in Scorpio and the 6th house suggests a past life working with enemies and aliens. Steven would have explored his own power before and then brought it into this life. The ability to influence millions through his films is an outward expression of using the kundalini power. He has learnt to use the power of Rahu Ketu positively.

The placement of Venus and Mars as the dispositors of Rahu Ketu is vital. Venus is in Libra in the 5th house of creativity giving it immense strength. It is placed in its own sign in one of the best houses and is regarded a positive planet for Gemini rising. The whole focus of Rahu in the 12th is therefore further enhanced. Mars is in Sagittarius, its friend's house. Mars is also placed in Mula, a Ketu nakshatra, further enhancing the Ketu influence. Venus is placed in the 11th house from Mars and Mars in the 3rd from Venus, so their relative placement is also positive.

As we look deeper into the nodes on this chart you can see that they are reinforced by every factor. The 12th house Rahu placement is considered negative but it is placed in Taurus, its exalted sign, making 12th house issues easier to manage. Its dispositor is also beneficially placed in its own sign.

Step Five - The Nakshatra Axis

The nakshatra placement of Rahu Ketu shows how the mind has been subtly influenced. Rahu is placed in Rohini and Ketu in Jyeshta. The Moon rules Rohini and Mercury rules Jyeshta highlighting struggles between the intellect and the intuition. As Rahu is in Rohini, it will be Rohini issues that dominate the physical aspects of life and Jyeshta issues that could be an intellectual block. One of the problems in analysing the nakshatra struggle in a celebrity chart is that it is of such a personal nature that you would need feedback to confirm how it is manifesting. However Spielberg's public struggles are emphasized from the nakshatras as well and of these we know more. Mercury, the nakshatra ruler of Ketu, is placed with Ketu itself showing a strong past life influence on his psyche. His ability to cut away from what he found difficult to deal with is shown in his initial rejection of his faith. Eventually he re-connected and the invisible link between himself and Judaism was re-established. This would have created great happiness from within.

Rahu in Rohini transports the soul to a new dimension and Spielberg has used this quality very creatively. Rohini's ruler, the Moon, is placed in the 5th house of creativity and entertainment and is placed with Jupiter. This forms an important planetary yoga called Gajakesari - the elephant and lion yoga, usually connected to a bright mind. Jyeshta shows a shift of the soul axis, but in a previous life. While the present life would be essentially materialistic, the ideas and the sense of destiny to make people aware of a world beyond their expectations, was formed from past experiences. Steven Spielberg has transported those ideas and given them form in this world.

Step Six - Navamsha

Navamsha is the ninth harmonic chart. The position of Rahu Ketu in the navamsha show how the nodes develop in the individual chart. It is also viewed as a chart for partnership. Again only one nodal position in the navamsha will be positive while the other will be more difficult. Rahu is placed in Gemini in the 4th house which is challenging, and Ketu is placed in Sagittarius in the positive 10th. Ketu is a multi-coloured energy and in the 10th it further illustrates his ability to be distinct and unusual. Rahu in the 4th may create issues with the mother. The 4th house is linked to happiness but Rahu there suggests a fear of never being totally happy. Mars conjuncts Rahu in the 4th house in the navamsha, and Mars rules Ketu in the rasi, all further enhancing the nodal influence.

In the navamsha Mercury and Jupiter are the nodal dispositors. Mercury which was the dispositor of Ketu in the Ascendant, now becomes the dispositor

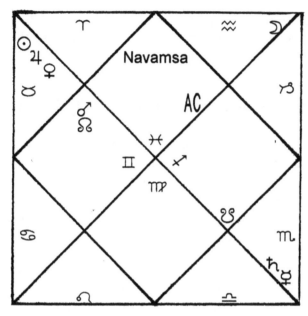

Steven Spielberg - Navamsha Chart

of Rahu. Mercury is vargottamma giving added strength to the nodes and in the navamsha it is placed in the lucky 9th house. Another important factor for Mercury is that although it sits on the tail of Ketu in the rasi, in the navamsha the nodes move into different signs, giving the intellect the power to see beyond the nodal turmoil.

Step Seven - Conjunctions

Steven Spielberg has a powerful conjunction of Mercury in the mouth of Ketu. Mercury is placed at 14 degrees 41' Scorpio. It is also the Ascendant ruler as was analysed in Step One. Mercury rules the 4th house indicating an unusual mother or an uneasy relationship with her. His mother was a trained pianist who instilled a love of music in her son. But creative people are not usually traditionalists and Steven was spoilt by his mother and usually got his own way. Others often saw her as flighty and childlike, but the Ketu Mercury combination does show that Spielberg felt a huge sense of rejection from his mother. His chart shows that his parents' divorce in 1966 would have affected him deeply. Mercury is also the significator of the mind and Mercury Ketu shows an abstract thinker, a person who goes beyond the usual mental constraints and thinks in a way that others do not understand. Steven Spielberg's mental ability to explore the strange and unusual is directly due to this conjunction.

Rahu does not conjunct any planet in the rasi chart; in the navamsha it is placed with Mars in Gemini in the 4th house creating further stress in the relationship with the mother. Mars also rules Ketu in the rasi, increases the nodal influence further.

Step Eight - The Influence of the Rahu Ketu Nakshatras

The nodes can influence the planets through their rulerships. For Spielberg the most significant influence is on the Moon at 13°44' Libra in the nakshatra of Swati ruled by Rahu - this means his first dasha was Rahu. The Moon signifies both his mind and mother so he would have been a fearful child and the relationship with his mother would have been complex. As a child he retreated into his mind which became a fertile place for development of future ideas and movies. Swati nakshatra shows a person who lives with stress and nervous tension. He can easily tire mentally but he also aspires to success and wealth, and the Moon in Swati gives him the ability to cut through competition. You can see this quality whenever one of his films is released - few competitors would now dare to bring their films out at the same time.

The Ascendant is 17°40' Gemini in the nakshatra of Ardra ruled by Rahu. This has already been discussed in Step One.

Both the Sun and Mars are placed in Mula. The Sun is at 3°20' and Mars is at 8°01', both in Sagittarius. Mula's influence on the Sun would create a subtle feeling of rejection from the father (the Sun being the significator of the father). Steven's father was an engineer and a workaholic who appeared to be emotionally distant but wanted his son to do well at school. Steven may feel that he has never lived up to the aspirations of his father, but the parents' divorce would have made Steven connect to his own strength more. Although he appears to be one of the leaders of movie making, there is a strong sense of inner spirituality that is expressed in his work. Mars in Mula gives him the ability to face his challenges with strength and courage, and Mars rules Ketu so there is a double Ketu influence.

Step Nine - Yogas

There are no Rahu Ketu yogas in this chart.

Step Ten - The Timing

The most important timing of the nodal experience is seen through the dasha patterns. Spielberg was born in a Rahu dasha, then in 1955 he began a Jupiter dasha, and Jupiter is conjunct the Rahu dispositor Venus. The Saturn dasha from 1971 is perhaps the only dasha where the nodal influence was restricted to their bhuktis. Then from 1990 he moved into a Mercury dasha, and Mercury is conjunct Ketu. After that he will enter the Ketu dasha in 2007. Everyone has to honour the nodes in their lives and Spielberg has demonstrated beautifully through his films how to face up to their power.

Rahu dasha

His first dasha, Rahu was prevalent from birth until June 3rd 1955. His formative years were influenced by Rahu, which as we've discussed, could not have been easy. With Rahu in the secret 12th house Spielberg felt isolated from his school mates and took refuge in the world of his imagination. Usually you would associate the 5th house with ideas but the 12th is the house of dreams and ideas that are detached from reality. However, the Rahu dispositor is placed in the 5th house, so both his dreams and ideas are connected here. The 5th house is also that of movies and entertainment so from a very young age Steven dreamt of being a film maker. He says he can always trace his movies to his childhood experiences: he enjoyed tormenting his sisters, and one of them said he had merely transferred terrifying them to terrifying the masses in 'Jaws', 'Poltergeist', 'Twilight Zone', 'Aracnophobia'...

• His most difficult period within the axis was the Rahu dasha Ketu bhukti (2nd December 1947 to 21st December 1948). As this happened when he was only a year old, he would probably not remember the experience, yet what was happening around him at that time would have profoundly affected him subconsciously.

Dasha and Bhukti start dates		
Rahu	Merc	12/18/1946
Rahu	Ketu	12/02/1947
Rahu	Ven	12/20/1948
Rahu	Sun	12/21/1951
Rahu	Moon	11/14/1952
Rahu	Mars	05/15/1954
Jup	Jup	06/03/1955
Jup	Sat	07/22/1957
Jup	Merc	02/02/1960
Jup	Ketu	05/10/1962
Jup	Ven	04/16/1963
Jup	Sun	12/15/1965
Jup	Moon	10/03/1966
Jup	Mars	02/02/1968
Jup	Rahu	01/07/1969
Sat	Sat	06/03/1971
Sat	Merc	06/06/1974
Sat	Ketu	02/13/1977
Sat	Ven	03/25/1978
Sat	Sun	05/25/1981
Sat	Moon	05/07/1982
Sat	Mars	12/06/1983
Sat	Rahu	01/14/1985
Sat	Jup	11/21/1987
Merc	Merc	06/03/1990
Merc	Ketu	10/30/1992
Merc	Ven	10/27/1993
Merc	Sun	08/27/1996
Merc	Moon	07/04/1997
Merc	Mars	12/03/1998
Merc	Rahu	11/30/1999
Merc	Jup	06/18/2002
Merc	Sat	09/23/2004
Ketu	Ketu	06/03/2007
Ketu	Ven	10/30/2007
Ketu	Sun	12/29/2008
Ketu	Moon	05/06/2009
Ketu	Mars	12/05/2009
Ketu	Rahu	05/03/2010
Ketu	Jup	05/22/2011
Ketu	Sat	04/27/2012
Ketu	Merc	06/06/2013
Ven	Ven	06/02/2014
Ven	Sun	10/03/2017
Ven	Moon	10/02/2018
Ven	Mars	06/03/2020
Ven	Rahu	08/02/2021
Ven	Jup	08/02/2024
Ven	Sat	04/03/2027
Ven	Merc	06/03/2030
Ven	Ketu	04/03/2033
Sun	Sun	06/02/2034
Sun	Moon	09/20/2034

• The Rahu dasha Mars bhukti from 5th May 1954 to 3rd June 1955 marked the challenging end of Rahu. This was when Spielberg was bullied at school and the period would prove to be significant.

Jupiter Dasha
The Jupiter dasha from 3rd June 1955 to 3rd June 1971 carried the influence of the nodes subtly as it was conjunct the dispositor of Rahu, Venus. It also ruled Ketu in the navamsha.

• The Jupiter dasha Venus bhukti ran from 14th April 1963 to 15th December 1965. Venus is the dispositor of Rahu. Spielberg's first feature length film 'Firelight' was shown on 24th March 1964 in Arizona. The name paid a subconscious homage to fiery Mars, the ruler of both Mercury and Ketu.

• The Jupiter dasha Mars bhukti ran from 2nd February 1968 to 7th January 1969. He had been serious about film making since the age of 12 and said his greatest ambition was to direct a film for a big studio before he was 20. Just before his 22nd birthday he was the youngest film maker to be contracted to a studio (Universal on 12th December 1968). Mars is the dispositor of Ketu.

• The Jupiter dasha Rahu bhukti ran from 7th Jan 1969 to 3rd June 1971. Rahu was exalted in the 12th house of dreams with its dispositor in the 5th connected to movies. At the start of this Rahu bhukti Spielberg was starting to fulfill his long-held dreams. The 12th house rulership suggests he would be working behind the scenes, but Rahu placed in the 8th house from Jupiter was a difficult position showing the ending of a way of life. By fulfilling his dreams he may also have been giving up his independence, and he dropped out of college on 31st January 1969 to begin work on his first TV programme for Universal.

Saturn dasha
The Saturn dasha ran from 3rd June 1971 to 3rd June 1990 and Saturn is the only planet that is not directly influenced by Rahu Ketu. So it was only during the bhuktis of Mercury, Ketu, Venus, Sun, Moon, Mars, Rahu, and Jupiter that he would experience the nodal influence. This was an extremely productive period for Spielberg as the hardworking Saturn tempered and enhanced the difficult nodal energy. It appears that during this Saturn dasha he was able to move outside the strong nodal impact of his life and use its energy productively.

• Saturn dasha Mercury bhukti ran from 6th June 1974 to 13th February 1977. Mercury's conjunction with Ketu activated the nodal influence in its bhukti.

The film 'Jaws' was released during this period in 1975. The symbolism connected to the nodes was of a demonic shark and people finally killing the demon to find peace. Spielberg said he made 'Jaws' as a way of facing his fears, as things never look so frightening when you faced them head on. Mercury was placed in the 5th house from the dasha ruler, Saturn. Another very successful film 'Close Encounters of the Third Kind' was released in 1977. He could have been in Saturn Mercury or Saturn Ketu at this time and both bhuktis show two sides of the same coin. This was going to be a very positive period of time when he brought his inner demons into light and exorcised them.

• Saturn dasha Ketu bhukti ran from 13th February 1977 to 25th March 1978. After the success of 'Close Encounters of the Third Kind' he experienced audience rejection for the first time with his comedy film '1941'. He soon went back to his exciting action films, which kept the audience on the edge of a thrilling experience - a very Rahu expression.

• Saturn dasha Venus bhukti ran from 25th March 1978 to 25th May 1981. During this time he directed 'Raiders of the Lost Ark' - a phenomenally successful movie. Venus is the dispositor of Rahu.

• The Saturn dasha Sun bhukti ran from 25th May 1981 to 7th May 1982. During this time he made 'E.T'. The Sun was in the Ketu ruled nakshatra of Mula, so the Ketu influence was very strong. Ketu lifts you above all competition like a flag raised aloft, and 'E.T.' confirmed Spielberg's place among the film greats. 'E.T.' also reflected a child's loneliness - taken from his own childhood with Rahu in the lonely 12th house. It also dealt with an innocent child connecting with a strange creature which the rest of the world feared and rejected. These are all nodal themes. 'E.T.' annihilated any competition and other films released at that time stood no chance - all due to Mercury and Ketu in the 6th.

Mercury dasha
The Mercury dasha began in 1990 and it continues Spielberg's extraordinary success story. His flag flies so high it is almost impossible for another person to emulate his success. Just when it was thought he could not do anything more, he came forward with 'Jurassic Park' in 1993, (the Mercury dasha Ketu bhukti). This Ketu bhukti also healed the ambivalent feelings he had with his Jewish roots with the excellent 'Schindler's List' which won him the much deserved Oscar for best director. He won another Oscar for 'Saving Private Ryan' in 1998.

• The Mercury Mars dasha began on 12th March 1998, ensuring his win over competitors. Mars disposits Mercury and Ketu. Then in the Mercury dasha Rahu bhukti in January 2001, he was given an honorary knighthood by Queen Elizabeth.

One of the important factors regarding Spielberg's phenomenal success is the sense of dissatisfaction that Rahu and Ketu bring with them. Most people would have been satisfied with the success he has enjoyed, but the nodal influence makes him unhappy and dissatisfied. With the success of each new film comes the feeling that he has only achieved a fraction of that of which he is capable. This drives him on to achieve yet more. It will be with the Ketu dasha, which begins on 3rd June 2007, that he is likely to start thinking about pursuing other agendas. When you are born with either the Rahu or Ketu dasha at birth, there is a possibility of experiencing the other half of your axis (as a dasha) during your lifetime. Usually this dasha allows you to come to terms with your axis issues and resolve your crisis. Spielberg's crisis appears to be the need to achieve unparalleled success, yet without exploring his inner self he will not find lasting satisfaction. He will have to find another mark by which to judge his achievements, and then he will be emotionally fulfilled.

Step Eleven - Transits

Rahu transits enhance your strengths. When the British Government announced on 1st January 2001 that Steven Spielberg was to be made an honorary knight, transiting Rahu was at 21°47' Gemini within 4° of his natal Ascendant. Transiting Ketu was also conjunct transiting Mercury at 21°25' Sagittarius within a few minutes. Mercury is both the natal Ascendant ruler and the present dasha ruler, so this was a powerful transit. Both the nodes were enhancing the quality of the Ascendant and re-inforcing the natal chart. Ketu transits usually highlight vulnerabilities. Ketu (in 2001) was transiting the house of relationship, indicating that while Steven Spielberg may have been receiving plaudits and honours on the international level, his relationship and marriage could have been going through a challenging time.

His parents' divorce in 1966

Steven Spielberg experienced his first nodal return on 27th June 1965. Transiting Ketu conjuncting the natal 4th house ruler Mercury, would have brought out in the open the problems his mother was experiencing. Ketu activated his vulnerable point. The nodes were still in the Taurus Scorpio axis when the divorce took place.

1982 - The Release of ET

On 14th August 1982 Rahu was exactly conjunct his Ascendant, pointing to the summer of 1982 as the time when the 'ET' phenomenon caught everyone's imagination and established Spielberg as the movie maker extraordinaire. Fast forward 18 years and Rahu again enhanced his already great reputation with a knighthood - possibly the ultimate accolade.

Meeting Amy Irving and Kate Capshaw

Steven first met Amy Irving in 1975/76 (date unknown). On 18th January 1976 transiting Rahu was conjunct natal Jupiter, the 7th house ruler, indicating the possibility of meeting a partner or lover. 2nd March 1984 was the 2nd nodal return and at this time he would have felt that a new episode had started in his life. He reunited with Amy Irving in 1984 and married her in 1985 during the Saturn Rahu dasha. He first met Kate Capshaw around 1983 when she was reading for 'Indiana Jones and the Temple of Doom' (released in 1984). Transiting Ketu was in his 7th house highlighting his vulnerability over relationships. Ketu obscures the real picture, creating illusions and making a person aspire for the perfect relationship. Both his main partnerships are connected to that transit of Ketu. Two planets are placed in the 7th indicating more than one relationship. Steven Spielberg may have been confused about who to chose as his life partner.

Step Twelve - Remedial Measures

As a person so governed by the nodes, it would be important for Spielberg to adopt the yogic breathing. As he lives life on the edge, the alternative breathing every day would be a great help to calm him down. Of the two nodal planets it is Ketu that conjuncts his Ascendant ruler and has the greater influence. He could try chanting the Ketu mantra. The image of Ganesha would be a help to further unlock any doors that are closed to him. As a man who has achieved so much, recognising his achievement and being content within himself would help in his happiness. He should try to pursue a spiritual path, not necessarily an Indian spirituality but one of his own. This would bring a peace of mind that I feel he lacks at present.

Vedic Astrology Basics

Tropical and Sidereal Zodiacs

Vedic astrology uses a combination of the solar and the lunar zodiacs. The solar zodiac is divided into twelve signs from Aries to Pisces, similar to the Western signs, but they are calculated in a different way. Western astrologers use the Sayana or tropical zodiac, which shows the Earth's relationship with the Sun, while vedic astrologers use the Nirayana, or sidereal zodiac, which is the planets' position relative to the stars. Sidereal actually means 'of the stars'.

Ayanamsha

The basis of the sidereal zodiac is the adoption of 285 AD as zero ayanamsha. This was the time when the tropical and the sidereal zodiacs were identical: the first degree of Aries, the vernal equinox point, was the same for both. The equinox point moves backwards due to the precession of the equinoxes with an annual motion of 50 seconds, and this difference - known as *ayanamsha* - is taken into account with the sidereal zodic, but not the tropical. There are many ayanamshas used by astrologers but the most acceptable one is the Lahiri which uses 285 AD as zero ayanamsha. The Lahiri ayanamsha is at present running about 23 degrees 49 minutes behind the tropical zodiac, so to draw up your vedic chart you need to subtract the ayanamsha from the tropical position of the planets and the Ascendant in your birth chart. Most western computer programmes will work it out exactly for you. The exact ayanamsha from 1900 is shown over the page.

The Lahiri Ayanamsha:

1/1/1900 - 22°27'55"
1/1/1910 - 22°35'45"
1/1/1920 - 22°44'37"
1/1/1930 - 22°52'35"
1/1/1940 - 23°01'16"
1/1/1950 - 23°09'28"
1/1/1960 - 23°17'53"
1/1/1970 - 23°26'21"
1/1/1980 - 23°34'31"
1/1/1990 - 23°43'14"
1/1/2000 - 23°51'11"

The Nakshatras - the Lunar Zodiac

The Indian Lunar zodiac is based on the Moon's movement against the backdrop of the stars as it makes its way around the zodiac each lunar month - it takes 27 days, 7 hours 43 minutes and 11.5 seconds for the Moon to return to its original position. This way of considering the relationship between the planets and stars divides the ecliptic into sections of 13°20', the distance travelled by the Moon in one solar day. The resultant 27 divisions are called nakshatras, and the placing of a planet within any nakshatra on the natal chart will have great bearing on the way its energies are utilised.

Each nakshatra is further divided into four parts known as *padas* or feet. The 27 nakshatras are divided in to 3 groups, known as pariyaya that means cycle. The seven planets and the nodes of the moon have the rulership assigned to each nakshatra. They repeat themselves in the same sequence. The 27 nakshatras are:

1. **Ashwini** - ruled by Ketu. 0°00' to 13°20' (0°00' to 13°20' Aries)
2. **Bharani** - ruled by Venus. 13°20' to 26°40' (13°20' to 26°40' Aries)
3. **Krittika** - ruled by the Sun. 26°40' to 40°00 (26°40' Aries to 10°00' Taurus)
4. **Rohini** - ruled by the Moon. 40°00' to 53°20' (10°00' to 23°20' Taurus)
5. **Mrigshira** - ruled by Mars. 53°20' to 66°40' (23°20' Taurus to 6°40' Gemini)
6. **Ardra** - ruled by Rahu. 66°40' to 80°00' (6°40' to 20°00' Gemini)
7. **Punarvasu** - ruled by Jupiter. 80°00' to 93°20' (20°00' Gemini to 3°20' Cancer)
8. **Pushya** - ruled by Saturn. 93°20' to 106°40' (3°20' to16°20' Cancer)

9. **Ashlesha** - ruled by Mercury. 106°40' to 120°00' (16°40' Cancer to 0°00' Leo)
10. **Magha** - ruled by Ketu. 120°00' to 132°20' (0°00' to 13°20' Leo)
11. **Purva Phalguni** - ruled by Venus. 132°20' to 146°40' (13°20' to 26°40' Leo)
12. **Uttara Phalguni** - ruled by the Sun. 146°40' to 160°00' (26°40' Leo to 10°00' Virgo)
13. **Hasta** - ruled by the Moon. 160°00' to 173°20' (10°00' to 23°20' Virgo)
14. **Chitra** - ruled by Mars. 173°20' to 186°40' (23°20' Virgo to 6°40' Libra)
15. **Swati** - ruled by Rahu. 186°40' to 200°00' (6°40' to 20°00' Libra)
16. **Vishakha**-ruled by Jupiter. 200°00' to 213°20' (20°00'Libra to 3°20' Scorpio)
17. **Anuradha** - ruled by Saturn. 213°20' to 226°40' (3°20' to 16°40'Scorpio)
18. **Jyeshta** - ruled by Mercury. 226°40' to 240°00' (16°40' Scorpio to 0°00' Sagittarius)
19. **Mula** - ruled by Ketu. 240°00' to 253°20' (0°00' to 13°20' Sagittarius)
20. **Purvashadha** - ruled by Venus. 253°20' to 266°40' (13°20' to 26°40')
21. **Uttarashadha** - ruled by the Sun. 266°40' to 280°00' (26°40' Sag to 10°00' Capricorn)
22. **Shravana** - ruled by the Moon. 280°00' to 293°20' (10°00' to 23°20' Capricorn)
23. **Dhanishta** - ruled by Mars. 293°20' to 306°40' (23°20' Cap to 6°40' Aquarius)
24. **Shatabhishak** - ruled by Rahu. 306°40' to 320°00' (6°40' to 20°00' Aquarius)
25. **Purva Bhadra** - ruled by Jupiter. 320°00' to 333°20' (20°00' Aquarius to 3°20' Pisces)
26. **Uttara Bhadra** - ruled by Saturn. 333°20' to 346°40' (3°20' to 16°40' Pisces)
27. **Revati** - ruled by Mercury. 346°40' to 360°00' (16°40' to 30°00' Pisces)

There is a 28th nakshatra called Abhijit, which is used in Mahurata (electional astrology) but is no longer used within the cycle of the nakshatras. Its position is from 276°40' to 280°54' and it takes over part of Uttara Ashadha and Shravana nakshatras.

Vargas - The Divisional Charts

The word *varga* means a part or division. Vargas are used in a specialised area of Jyotish which assesses a variety of charts arrived at by dividing a whole zodiac sign (30⁰) by different numbers. The *rasi* (natal) chart is a varga chart: the 30⁰ divided by one. If your rasi chart represents your whole outer personality in all its complexity, each varga chart represents a particular area of your life writ large: it takes a theme already present in the rashi chart and magnifies it for closer study. Navamsha is the most important varga that is studied by vedic astrologers.

Navamsha - Nine Divisions of a Sign (3°20' each)

This is the one varga chart that a vedic astrologer would automatically use when preparing for a consultation with a client. It is particularly helpful in relationship astrology. It highlights the issues of the auspicious ninth house: what positive karma you will be able to call on during this lifetime, what level of happiness you might expect; and what future is indicated for you. The navamsha chart reflects the inner self that will deal with the material and spiritual challenges encountered by the outer self. It can show what inner resources you will have; whether there will be conflict between your inner and outer self over how to resolve difficult issues, and how your inner self will be affected by life's ups and downs. It also shows your personal development and the areas you may be reaching towards in your life, but which may be causing you stress because you haven't got to them yet. The navamsha chart represents our future as it is something we 'grow into'. It is calculated in two steps: first find which division of 3°20' the planet or Ascendant falls into on the rasi chart and note its navamsha number (see table). Next find the cardinal sign in the same element - this is where you will count from.

Degree	Navamsha
00°00' to 03°20'	1st
03°20' to 06°40'	2nd
06°40' to 10°00'	3rd
10°00' to 13°20'	4th
13°20' to 16°40'	5th
16°40' to 20°00'	6th
20°00' to 23°20'	7th
23°20' to 26°40'	8th
26°40' to 30°00'	9th

The navamsha begins with each sign being divided into 9 divisions or vargas. Rulerships begin with the ruler of the cardinal sign in the same element, as in this list:

Sign being subdivided	Rulership begins with
Aries, Leo, Sagittarius	Mars (Aries)
Taurus, Virgo, Capricorn	Saturn (Capricorn)
Gemini, Libra, Aquarius	Venus (Libra)
Cancer, Scorpio, Pisces	Moon (Cancer)

As an example, consider Venus at 10°20' Aquarius. From the first table we see that it falls into the 4th navamsha section. Aquarius is an air sign, and we find from the second table that the cardinal air sign is Libra. Count four signs on starting from Libra, which brings us to Capricorn - so in the navamsha chart Venus is in Capricorn.

Glossary

Benefic - positive planet
Bhukti - planetary subdivision of a mahadasha
Dasha - direction or planetary system of predicting
Chayya Grahas - shadow planets
Dispositor - planet that rules the sign where a planet is placed
Dushtana - enemy or difficult houses
Gandanta - certain degrees that have karmic significance
Guna - psychological qualities of Sattva, Rajas and Tamas
Karaka - significator
Kendras - the cardinal houses (1st, 4th, 7th and 10th)
Lagna - ascendant
Mahadasha - main planetary period
Malefic - negative planet
Moksha - self-realisation
Mooltrikona - special degrees where planets become very powerful
Nakshatra - the name given to a group of stars
Prayantara - the planetary subdivision of the bhukti
Purva punya - good deeds from past life
Raja yoga karaka - a planet that signifies success. (Venus for Capricorn and Aquarius
     Ascendant, Mars for Cancer and Leo, Saturn for Taurus and Libra).
Rajas - the quality of action, search and agitation
Sahasara - the crown chakra
Sattva - the quality of purity and truth
Significator - indicator
Sub-dashas - also known as bhukti, they are the secondary period in a maha dasha
Tamas - the quality of darkness, laziness, earthly attachments
Triplicity - triple influences
Varga - divisions of the birth chart that are specifically used in vedic astrology
Vargottoma - when a planet is in the same sign in both the rasi and navamsha charts

Further Reading

The Essentials of Vedic Astrology, Komilla Sutton. The Wessex Astrologer, England.
Rahu & Ketu in Predictive Astrology, Manik Chand Jain. Sagar Publications, India.
The Mystery of Rahu in a Horoscope, Shiv Raj Sharma. Sagar Publications, India.
Nakshatras, Dennis M. Harness PH.D. Lotus Press, U.S.A.
Starting Yoga, Doriel Hall. Ward Lock Ltd, England
Healing Yoga, Swami Ambikananda Saraswati. Marlowe and Co. USA
The Principles of Breathwork Swami Ambikananda Saraswati. Thorsons, England
Meditation, Eknath Easwaran. Penguin, England

Reference Text

Varahamihira's Brihat Samhita. Translated by M. Ramakrishna Bhat

Schools and Organisations

American Council of Vedic Astrology (ACVA)
PO Box 2149
Sedona, AZ 86339
Tel: (520) 282 6595   Email: acva@sedona.net
The Institute of Vedic Astrology also operates from this address. For course information contact Dennis Harness at DMHarness@aol.com

British Association for Vedic Astrology (BAVA)
19, Jenner Way
Romsey
Hants
SO51 8PD
Tel: + 44 (0)1794 524178 Email: bava@btinternet.com   Website: www.bava.org

Dirah Academie
Brunostraat 64B
NL 5042 JA Tilburg
The Netherlands
Tel: + 31 13 463 5468

Indian Council of Astrological Sciences
64 Gowdiamutt Road
Royapeeta
Madras 600 014
India

Northeast Institute of Vedic Astrology and Studies
854 Brock Avenue
New Bedford MA 02744
Tel 1 508 990 7898   Email crystalx@ici.net

NW Institute of Vedic Sciences
7212 Woodlawn Avenue NE
Seattle, WA 98115
Tel: (206) 525 2229

Computer Software

Shri Jyoti Star Software
Shri Source, Barn Cottage
Brooklands Farm Close
Kilmington, Devon
EX13 7SZ
England
Website www.vedicsoftware.com

Goravani Jyotish
211 Crest Drive,
Eugene, OR 97405
USA
Tel 001 541 485 8453
Website: www.gorovani.com

Index

BOOKS PUBLISHED
OR DISTRIBUTED BY US INCLUDE:

THE COSMIC LOOM -   £15.95
DENNIS ELWELL

ASTROLOGY AND KABBALAH -   £12.95
Z'EV BEN SHIMON HALEVI

THE HOROSCOPE IN MANIFESTATION (IN PAPERBACK) -   £15.99
LIZ GREENE

WORKING WITH ASTROLOGY -   £14.95
MIKE HARDING AND CHARLES HARVEY

ORPHEUS -   £14.99
EDITED BY SUZI HARVEY

THE ESSENTIALS OF VEDIC ASTROLOGY -   £13.99
KOMILLA SUTTON

PATTERNS OF THE PAST -   £12.50
JUDY HALL

ASTROLOCALITY ASTROLOGY -   £12.50
MARTIN DAVIS

THE CONSULTATION CHART -   £14.50
WANDA SELLAR

AND MANY, MANY MORE.......

THE WESSEX ASTROLOGER

For a full list of titles please see our website or contact us at:
PO Box 2751, Bournemouth BH6 3ZJ, England.
Tel/Fax +44 (0)1202 424695.

www.wessexastrologer.com

Also by Komilla Sutton

The Essentials

of

Vedic Astrology

£13.99   ISBN 1902405064

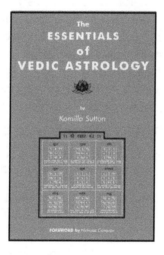

'Komilla's book is perhaps the easiest and most comprehensive introduction to vedic astrology for beginnners'

Andrew Foss, co-founder of the British Association for Vedic Astrology